SIDEWALKS, SACRISTIES, AND SINNERS

Stories of Living Faith

John McGowan, C.SS.R.

LIGUORI
PUBLICATIONS

One Liguori Drive
Liguori, Missouri 63057
(314) 464-2500

This book is for Chris who stood
in the back of the church and
listened to my many stories while
all the time his smile, his love,
and his life were telling the
best story of all.

Imprimi Potest:
Stephen T. Palmer, C.SS.R.
Provincial, St. Louis Province
Redemptorist Fathers

Imprimatur:
+ Edward J. O'Donnell
Vicar General, Archdiocese of St. Louis

ISBN 0-89243-283-7
Library of Congress Catalog Card Number: 87-83613

Cover photos by:
L. George/H. Armstrong Roberts
and
R. Lloyd/H. Armstrong Roberts

Copyright © 1988, Liguori Publications
Printed in U.S.A.

TABLE OF CONTENTS

Preface 5

1. A Surprise for "Mamma" 7

2. The Twelve Green Socks 13

3. A Sandwich Story 18

4. Michael's Last Summer 27

5. An Emmaus Story 34

6. The Days of Wine and Aldo 40

7. Charlie's Promise 45

8. Meghan! 50

9. Words of Wisdom
   From Joe the Engraver 54

10. Louis 60

11. Margaretta's View 65

12. The Deaths of Mike Hayden 70

13. The Man With God's Ear 75

PREFACE

This is a *Story Book*. To be more precise, it is a "spin-off" of the Gospels. The only difference between the two is that the tellers of these tales are parishioners — men and women of a large Redemptorist parish in Brooklyn, New York. They are young people, old people, ethnic people, funny people, wounded people, searching people. They are the rejected and the redeemed, the dejected and the converted, the peasant and the priest. They stroll sidewalks, wait in check-out lines, sit in funeral homes, stare out kitchen windows, and speak stories to one another. In one way these people are very different from one another, but in another way they are very similar. They are all storytellers.

These people stop Father John as he goes through his day and they tell him their stories. He listens and laughs and responds. But later at night in his room, he reflects on all that he has seen and heard. In his silence he once again realizes that what he has heard that day is the Gospel — that never-ending story of life, death, and resurrection. In a very real way, Father John bumped into Lazarus or the rich young man or the widow of Nain or the boy possessed by demons. And he even met Jesus himself —dressed in today's threads and sputtering in this century's sounds, but Jesus all the same. Father John sees that the faces of his day belong to the Gospel people of the 1980s and their words and actions echo an answer of a long-ago Jesus to another John: "Go and tell John what you have seen and heard" (Luke 7:22).

This book contains dozens of story people: evangelists who do not dress in Gospel garments or wear veils on their heads or sandals on their feet or even long biblical beards. These people dwell in lonely living rooms or sleep in dirty hallways or wait out their days in chrome and plastic institutions. They are spitting images of the crowds who stopped Jesus of Nazareth and allowed him to parable them. They step out of the pages of Matthew, Mark, Luke, or John in their designer clothes. They constantly remind us that even to this day the Gospel is still spinning. They show us that Jesus of Nazareth is still alive and that we, all of us, are Gospel people with loads of good stories to share and good news to pass on.

For Father John, the best part is that the Gospel story and all the story-telling people live on in the lives of every one of us. It's only up to us to connect our story with the Jesus of Nazareth story. One way to do that these days is by reading that story in the words, faces, and lives of today's people. It is hoped that the readers recognize the Gospel people within these pages, but more especially the ones who walk and talk their journey to the kingdom.

This storyteller offers deepest gratitude to Marie who listened for hours to all his talked-out tales long before a single word hit paper; to Mary who proofread, corrected the manuscript, and offered many helpful suggestions; to Lucille for all her typing; and to all the people of Our Lady of Perpetual Help parish who called and encouraged him to keep the stories coming. Most of all, he thanks all the Gospel people who live inside these pages. By coming to him in the flesh with their stories, they made the WORD become Flesh once more. For that he is forever grateful!

"He spoke to them only in parables" (Matthew 13:34).

John McGowan, C.SS.R.

1

A SURPRISE
FOR "MAMMA"

While he [Jesus] was still speaking to the crowds, his mother and his brothers appeared outside, wishing to speak with him. [Someone told him, "Your mother and your brothers are standing outside, asking to speak with you."] But he said in reply to the one who told him, "Who is my mother? Who are my brothers?" And stretching out his hand toward his disciples, he said, "Here are my mother and my brothers. For whoever does the will of my heavenly Father is my brother, and sister, and mother" (Matthew 12:46-50).

The people filed past Father John on their way out of church; most smiled, some good-morninged him, others shook his hand. It was Sunday and the Mass was over. All the adult parishioners looked like summer in flowered print blouses or golf shirts with a little penguin, fox, or alligator on their pockets. Father John glistened in his green gothics like a just-sprayed, overgrown, hothouse plant. A handful of worshipers, the central air conditioning, and Tommy, the organist, sang along together, all praising the Lord "for our health and salvation."

"When are you going to come over to see Mamma?" A middle-aged woman locked her hand in his.

"How's she doing?"

"She's at home most of the time now. I get her up to church maybe for Christmas or Easter, but other than that she's stuck in the house." The priest remembered the woman's mother. She used to wave at him from the alcove and he would go over and make her laugh. "Mamma's in her eighties now. Why not drop in someday? She wants confession."

Father John smiled. The woman made wanting confession sound like "Mamma wants a container of milk and a half-dozen buns." "What's the address again?" He ripped a corner from a Sunday bulletin and scribbled some numbers on it.

"We're on the second floor. Come anytime. I work all day but Mamma's always there. She'll be glad to see you. Bring Jesus too!" He smiled again. She makes it sound like a shopping trip, "Bring one Jesus, one confession, and a pound of potatoes."

More people interrupted them so he unconsciously stuffed Mamma's address on the torn piece of bulletin into his pocket. The address roomed there along with a broken plastic rosary, some coins, and his tiny appointment book. It was three weeks before he found it again while reaching for a quarter to put in a parking meter. Mamma's address! He did not even know the old woman's name, but the number of the house and street accusingly stared up at him, making him feel awful and guilty. Once again he resolved to drop in to see Mamma someday.

The worn corner of the bulletin with the lonely numbers on it eventually found a home on his desk. It lived there for a while along with phone messages, books, old letters, and a few pens. At one time the Bible itself rested on top of it. Other notes and envelopes and scraps of paper marched off the desk to the wastepaper basket, but Mamma's address somehow sat there in the midst of rulers and paper clips and priestly paraphernalia until one August morning, when the priest decided to clean off the top of his desk. He picked it up and could almost feel it bite him. If you have time to clean your desk, he thought, you have time to visit "Mamma." So down he went to the rectory chapel, got the holy water and the ritual book from his drawer over the vestment case and opened the tabernacle to place the Eucharistic Lord in the Communion pyx. "Mamma, I'm on my way." He smiled to himself and walked down the rectory steps into the warm August sunshine. "One Jesus, one confession, and me!"

When he reached Ninth Avenue, he turned up one of the tree-shaded streets. Cars lined up on one side of the block, while the other curb waited patiently for the sanitation truck and its big brooms. It was so hot that only a few children were out playing. One or two adults eyed him fearfully as he walked along. Seeing a priest in black walking down a street still scared many people. Someone was dead or dying, they thought.

He finally reached Mamma's house. It was a nice, two-family house with a closed-in porch downstairs, flowers in a small front yard. He walked up the three steps and pushed the top bell. There he stood facing a closed door while all the windows on the block, with unseen eyes behind them, wondered what was wrong. No answer. He pushed the button again. Even if Mamma was up there, how in the world was she going to get down the stairs to let him in? He tried the door. Locked. No doubt everyone on the whole block was thinking that the poor old lady in the house was dead. He could feel their eyes on the back of his neck. Should have called first, he thought.

He rang again. Nothing. He backed down the steps and looked up. Over the closed-in porch of the first floor was a balcony where people could sit out. Maybe Mamma was sitting up there. He was going to call her but he didn't even know her name and he couldn't very well call out "Mamma." That would really upset the neighbors. Better go back to the rectory and call on the phone, he mused. So he came down the steps, looked up once more, and began to walk away.

"Hey, Father, Father!" A small Italian man was coming down the street. The priest turned around to face him. "You come to see the old lady upstairs?"

"Yes, but I get no answer."

"Come with me. I'll let you in. I live downstairs. She's too old to come to the door."

The man took out his keys for the front door. He led the priest into a beautiful foyer with a carpeted staircase leading upstairs. The priest entered while the man shouted in Italian up the stairs. Then he said in English, "The Father is here."

The door above opened, filling the landing with daylight. Mamma stepped out. She looked puzzled but Father John started up to her. "Hello, Mamma. I came over to see you." At that moment her mouth opened wide and all the lines on her motherly face smiled. She held out her chubby arms in welcome, making the priest feel like a small boy running to the embrace of his mother. He could see her eyes water with gladness.

"You come to see me!" She could hardly believe it. "Oh, please, come up, Father. Come up." She hugged him at the top of the stairs, then took his hand and led him into her apartment. "Excuse me. I heard the bell but I didn't know who it was."

They entered the dining room. Mamma shut the door and snapped the two locks. Then she turned around, reached her hands up behind Father John's head and pulled it down to give him a kiss. She was delirious with joy.

"I met your daughter in church a few weeks ago. She asked me to come over to see you."

"Oh, thank you, Father. Here, sit." Father John sat on a dining room chair while Mamma looked around the rooms and cleared this and that. "Please excuse the house. I didn't know you were coming."

"It's fine, Mamma. It's beautiful, just like you." He pulled over a dining room chair for her.

"It's not beautiful! It's a mess." She sat across from him, her back to the door, and smiled radiantly. She was dressed in a robe and was barefooted. "It's so good to see you!" Her puffy hands went between her knees and she squeezed the knees together.

"How are you feeling, Mamma?"

"Not so good. I can't even do the housework anymore."

"Don't worry about that!" The priest smiled at her and she looked so old, so tired, but so happy to have company — like a little girl at her birthday party.

"How's everything in the church? I miss it so much. Every day I used to go to Mass, make the visits, light the candles. Now I can't even go on Sundays." Her eyes filled up again; this time with sad tears. "I pray every day to God to help me. But even saying my prayers hurts. It's getting so hard."

She spoke on in her low, guttural voice, even lifting her hands at times to bring God into the conversation. She talked about being a little girl in Italy and working to help her mother and father raise a large family. She spoke of coming to this country. She spoke of marriage and a husband, long since buried. Words of pain, sickness, children, family — they all ran on top of one another, some in English, some in Italian, some in the language of prayer. She told her story to the priest. And he sat in silence watching her, uh-huhing her now and then with a nod. Her eyes closed at times as she spoke, and occasionally Father John felt like an intruder in a conversation between God and the old woman.

Her gray hair was short and uncombed. Her neck and chin pouched together to join the rest of her small, round body. Father John just watched her. Her watery eyes were still beautiful and really told him her story of days and people no longer present. She was not complaining, merely remembering out loud and bouncing her pain and loneliness off him.

After a while, Father John asked her if she would like to go to confession. She joined her hands and devoutly confessed the sins of a saint. "Now, Mamma, how about Communion?"

Her face almost glowed. "You brought the Communion?"

He took the gold pyx from his shirt pocket and placed it on the table. Together they prayed the prayer that Jesus gave us and he then stood before her and said, "This is the Lamb of God who takes away the sins of the world. Happy are those who are called to his supper." She opened her small mouth and he placed the host on her tongue. Then silence. Her head bent forward, with her round little fingers screening her closed eyes. The tiny, simple wedding band winked at the priest. He sat back down and allowed her to speak her story in silence to her Eucharistic visitor. It was a conversation just between the two of them and Father John respected their silent love words.

He stood again and sprinkled the top of her head with the holy water. She crossed herself, kissed the tips of her fingers, and clasped his hands in hers, like a gentle vise.

"Thank you so much, Father, for your visit. Wait till I tell my daughter you were here. She won't believe me." She got up and gave him a hug, her head as high as his chest. "You come again! Yes?"

"Yes, Mamma, I'll be back. You take care of yourself. And be good."

"Be good? What else can I do? It was such a nice visit. So good to see someone."

He opened the door and assured her that he would get down the stairs and let himself out. She stood on the landing, waving and God-blessing him all the way to the street. The hot sidewalk warmed his feet. What a nice visit, he thought. What a nice old lady. He walked back to the rectory, happy to be alive and happy for the visit. He was smiling all the way up the block.

2

THE TWELVE
GREEN SOCKS

When the hour came, he [Jesus] took his place at table with the apostles. He said to them, "I have eagerly desired to eat this Passover with you before I suffer, for, I tell you, I shall not eat it [again] until there is fulfillment in the kingdom of God." Then he took a cup, gave thanks, and said, "Take this and share it among yourselves; for I tell you [that] from this time on I shall not drink of the fruit of the vine until the kingdom of God comes." Then he took the bread, said the blessing, broke it, and gave it to them, saying, "This is my body, which will be given for you; do this in memory of me." And likewise the cup after they had eaten, saying, "This cup is the new covenant in my blood, which will be shed for you" (Luke 22:14-20).

From the crack of creation people have joined together in clubs and communities, in families and fraternities. We like to be alone now and then but more often than not we yearn to belong to some group. And we love to wear an insignia, an emblem, a tattoo, a scar, a uniform — anything that will advertise our bonding. Jesus had his crowd break bread and share a cup of wine together; and this, along with their love for one another, tipped them off to the rest of the world as Christians. The Three Musketeers crossed their swords together and shouted "All for one and one for all!" Franciscans, Dominicans, Redemptorists, and scores of other religious Orders wear unique outfits or habits as their I.D. Most of us label our jackets, shirts, or hats with letters or logos that bellow our belonging. Rings, secret signs, and passwords are a lot less messy than cutting our wrists and allowing our blood to mix with other blood brothers and sisters. So we proudly wear our TONY'S PIZZERIA BOCCHI BALL T-shirts and go to sleep each night and wake up each day assured that we belong, that we are not alone.

One particular group of friends selected green socks as their symbol of friendship. Why green socks? Well, it all came about casually and rather humorously. This particular band of buddies began as four married and two single men. They came together socially with wives and families a few times a year. At one of their Christmas gatherings, one of the single friends gifted the wives of the group with colorful plastic bracelets. The married members of this merry melange moaned and mocked the bracelet giver. "How come we never get a present?" they teased. "Why is it that the women always get gifted?" The bracelet giver kept the jeers and taunts in mind until their next gathering which happened to be March 17, the evening of St. Patrick's Day. With the entire group sitting in a circle in his living room, he reached into the drawer of an end table and tossed a pair of green socks at each man present. "Here!" he said, "don't say I never give you anything." Each man smiled and held up his green socks for all to see. Not only were the socks green, they were also embroidered with white shamrocks and white Irish pipes. The women, of course, laughed and clapped for the men to put them on. So off came their shoes and socks and on went their new green socks.

"This will be the sign of our solidarity," cried one. "We'll wear these socks every year at this time," added another.

"We'll wear them whenever we come together," bested a third. The cheers and the laughter increased and the twelve feet in green, with white pipes and shamrocks, touched soles and toes in the center of the circle. And in that unique position, they even posed for a picture. It was indeed a happy evening and when they parted to their homes and rooms and tossed their green socks into their hampers, they hardly realized how important a symbol of their friendship those twelve green socks would become.

In the years ahead, the twelve green socks would find themselves together in restaurants and living rooms and parish dances. One wearer would look at another wearer and ask, "You have them on?" The other would smile, pinch his trousers at the knee and pull up on the crease to reveal a green sock in July or a white shamrock in September. The wearing, the asking, the showing became the matter, the words, and the form of their secular sacrament of the green socks.

In time the twelve socks walked to the altar sacraments. They all attended a daughter's wedding one hot June day. Their biggest get-together happened on the day the actual giver of the green socks got married. On that day two green socks covered the groom's nervous feet. Four more green socks, inside ushers' shoes, walked up and down the aisle showing guests to their seats. Two more green socks absorbed the sweat off the feet of a nervous lector. Two more hid in secret anonymity in the body of the church and two more touched the wiggling toes of the celebrant on the altar witnessing the marriage vows. That was the happiest day by far for the twelve green socks and the twelve feet within them and the six friends wearing them.

Their next sacramental appearance together came a year later, not at another wedding but at the Baptism of their recently married friend's newborn daughter. The twelve green socks got really exhausted that day and with all the dancing, an occasional toenail wore through the reinforced toes. The twelve green socks on the twelve dancing feet of the six friends, who leaned over to kiss the brand-new baby, became the blessed bond of their love and friendship with one another. And farthest from the minds of any of the six friends was the fact that, within the space of less than a year, they would be wearing their green socks again, only this time at the funerals of two members of the group.

Up until those two dreadful occasions, the wearing of the green socks had been reserved for laughter, for dancing, for holidays, and happy sacraments. But on one late November Wednesday, ten green socks came together in sadness because the other two of them were on their friend in the coffin. The priest wore his, the lectors wore theirs, the other silent friends wore theirs, not because of a secret and silly camaraderie, but in memory of a friend who no longer walked with them. They wore their green socks that day in tribute to their friend who now walked with his barefooted Lord.

The following August another green-sock wearer suddenly walked off into eternity. And on that sunny Saturday, the eight green socks gathered once again in grief. This time two green socks covered the lifeless feet of their friend lying in the church's middle aisle, and eight other green socks, in some unique yet beautiful gesture, shouted ''We love you'' from the four remaining friends.

Green socks. They began as a tease, grew into a joke, became a ritual, but now are living memories of two departed friends. Green socks. Silly, ordinary, even gaudy, yet in some holy way they serve as vivid reminders that life is a *walk*. It's a stroll, a process, a journey. And the four living friends wearing their eight green socks know now more than ever before that they, too, are walking each day and getting closer to the Man with no socks, the barefoot, sandaled Man, who at this moment is on an endless walk with their two friends of the green socks.

And the four living friends, wearing the eight green socks, know that one day there will be only six green socks left. They also know that on another day there will be only four green socks left. But each one believes that the number will never get down to zero — not really. Because if it ever does, then that will be the glorious now in some distant and beautiful eternity when the twelve green socks will be together again. And when that happens, the six friends will be forever and what a happy forever that will be.

3
A SANDWICH STORY

While he [Jesus] was saying these things to them, an official came forward, knelt down before him, and said, "My daughter has just died. But come, lay your hand on her, and she will live." Jesus rose and followed him, and so did his disciples. A woman suffering hemorrhages for twelve years came up behind him and touched the tassel on his cloak. She said to herself, "If only I can touch his cloak, I shall be cured." Jesus turned around and saw her, and said, "Courage, daughter! Your faith has saved you." And from that hour the woman was cured.

When Jesus arrived at the official's house and saw the flute players and the crowd who were making a commotion, he said, "Go away! The girl is not dead but sleeping." And they ridiculed him. When the crowd was put out, he came and took her by the hand, and the little girl arose. And news of this spread throughout all that land (Matthew 9:18-26).

Scripture scholars refer to quotations like the above as "sandwich stories." A Jewish official asks Jesus to make a house call so he can lay his hand on the man's suddenly deceased daughter. On the Lord's way to the official's home, a woman suffering for twelve years with a hemorrhage touches the hem of his garment and she is cured. Jesus spends some time chatting with the woman about her faith. Then he continues on to the little girl's room, takes hold of her hand and, wouldn't you know it, she comes alive! One miracle is ''sandwiched'' between the beginning and the end of another.

Sandwich stories still occur in our Gospel days. Like the tasty items we pack between two slices of bread, lots of interesting, often exciting, occasionally curious, and sometimes miraculous incidents get sandwiched between our comings and goings. Take summer wakes, for example. A parishioner passes away and the family longs for a priest to come just to say a prayer and lay a hand on their beloved. What looks at the start to be a night at a wake turns into a treasury of tales or, better yet, a club sandwich filled with people, places, and pleas. ''Have you had lunch yet? Well, sit down and enjoy this *sandwich story.*''

Father John knew he had to get to the wake on this particular night or he wouldn't get there at all. A young husband and father had just lost a tough battle to cancer, leaving behind a young wife and an eleven-year-old daughter. If he couldn't offer a miracle, Father John thought, at least he could offer his presence, his prayers, and some comfort. So he wrote out a Mass card in the rectory office, buttoned the top of his black shirt, and slid the white plastic collar into the slot. ''I'm going over to the wake, Tom. I'll be right back'' were the last words he called to Brother Tom as he dashed out the door. He wouldn't see the Brother again until the next morning.

Father John got as far as the rectory stoop when five Hispanic teenagers greeted him with ''Hey, Father John, you're just the one we're looking for. We need a hall on these dates for our meetings.'' After chatting back and forth about the days and times of the meetings, Father scratched some additional scribbles on the paper. "I'll see what I can do. Gotta go. Be good!"

"You too!" one of them retorted. "Thanks, Father John. Where are you going?"

"To a wake," Father called back, as he took the rectory steps two at a time.

"Oh, good!" the boy responded. "Have a good time." Father John smiled inside at his response. Guess he doesn't know what a wake is, he thought. He got only as far as the side door of the lower church when he spotted four of his prize altar boys crossing the street toward him. They looked troubled.

"What's happening?" Father asked them.

"Hey, Father John" — the big one was to be the spokesman — "this lady on the block is gonna complain to you about us. She says we're buggin' her but we didn't do nuthin', honest."

"Baloney!" Father John interrupted. "Stop bugging the old people on the block. You have to respect the older people. What did you do?"

"She says we're shooting BB guns at her but there are no BBs in the gun and she said we set off firecrackers outside her house."

Father John took a deep breath. All of a sudden he found himself in the role of peace negotiator as the house-dressed woman came across the street. In no time at all, everyone was talking at once and there he was in the thick of it. "She said, I said, you did, no I didn't, yes you did" and all the usual expressions rose above the finger-pointing huddle. What am I doing here? Father John thought. I'm not their mother.

Finally, using his best weapon — his volume — Father John boomed above the disintegrating peace talk. "Quiet! Say you're sorry. Don't do it again and be nice to older people. Respect them or I'll beat you all up!" Oddly enough, they all laughed, even the lady in the housedress. "Look, I'd love to stay and iron this out with you but I have to go to a wake." Like a big league umpire,

Father John broke away and the off-duty altar boys and house-dressed woman wandered back to their positions on the block to continue the game of living. Two car lengths later he passed a mother and daughter playing stoop ball against a father and son. The family called to him and asked him if he wanted to play, but all he could do was repeat the words he had been saying all night: "Can't! I've got to go to a wake."

On the avenue he caught up with two parishioners, a woman from the Ladies Auxiliary and a Holy Name man, also on their way to the funeral home. The three of them walked along chatting cheerfully when, from the other direction, a tall man in a once white T-shirt weaved toward them. Oh, no! Father John thought. A handout and I have no money with me. The weaving T-shirt stopped before them. " 'Scuse me, Padre. Can I ask you a question?" Why do these guys always ask permission to ask a question with a question?

So with Harry Holy Name on one side of him and Linda Ladies Auxiliary on the other, Father John looked Tommy T-shirt right in the eye and lied. "Sure! Ask whatever you wish."

"Do I have a chance?" Tommy T-shirt obviously had been working on a few beers.

"A chance for what?" Father John asked.

"A chance to be forgiven!" Tommy T-shirt, like a tall flagpole, seemed to move in the wind.

"Forgiven for what?" Another question from Father John.

"Well, I'm forty-five years old and I haven't been to confession in over thirty years. My father was a policeman — he's dead now — and my mother prays for me every day. Do I have a chance?"

"Sure you have a chance!" all three of them answered together — Father John, Harry Holy Name, and Linda Ladies Auxiliary.

"Padre, can I ask you a question? How do I know that if I went to confession, the priest wouldn't throw me out?"

"If you were sick and went to see a doctor, would the doctor throw you out of his office because you were sick?"

"No . . . I guess not," Tommy answered.

"Then neither would a priest throw you out of confession."

"But it's thirty years, Padre. The priest would kill me."

"Look, I'm a priest and you told me. I didn't kill you, did I?"

"No" . . . Tommy was pondering that one when Linda Ladies Auxiliary spoke up in a beautiful and caring Irish brogue. "Look, son, do you ever say an Act of Contrition?"

"What's that?" Tommy swayed from side to side.

"O my God, I am heartily sorry for all my sins . . . " Linda said the prayer for Tommy. "Say that every night and then maybe someday you'll get the courage to go to the church for confession."

Father John smiled at Linda, feeling glad she was there with him when Harry Holy Name spoke up, giving Tommy the exact schedule for confession, both the times and days. This was a real three-on-one, Father John thought. Maybe we can get through to this guy. There was a long pause.

"Padre, can I ask you a question? You really think I have a chance?"

"Sure you do!" the three of them chorused in three-part harmony.

"But you have to make the move" Father John answered alone.

Tommy T-shirt smiled and scratched his two-day whiskers. "That's beautiful. You're a beautiful priest. I could kiss you."

"Not here," Father John smiled. "We'll all get arrested." They all answered with laughter that suddenly died when Tommy once again said, "I hate to keep you but can I ask you a question?" Each of Tommy's eyes looked in a different direction. "Is there a chance for me?"

"Yes, definitely," Father John came in fast. "God nudges all of us but we have to respond. The ball's in your court now. Hit it back and get to confession.'' Again another long pause during which Father John noticed that the daylight had all but disappeared and it was now night. Would he ever get to that wake, he wondered. Tommy reached out and grabbed Father's hand and held it. ''I'll think about it. You're beautiful. I trust you. I respect you. Forgive me for being blasphemous.'' The two hands shook up and down, up and down. Finally Tommy let go and swayed into the delicatessen.

The three disciples — Father John, Harry Holy Name, and Linda Ladies Auxiliary — stood there motionless for a moment before continuing to the funeral parlor. Father smiled at his companions, ''You guys did great. Who knows? We might have made an impression on him.''

''I don't think so, Father,'' Linda said. ''Here he comes again.'' With that the door of the delicatessen shot open and Tommy T-shirt strolled out with a six-pack under his arm. Not even giving a glance to the three disciples, he breezed past them as though he never saw them before and zigzagged up the avenue. The three disciples shrugged and slowly walked to the funeral parlor.

Father John did not get one foot into the parlor before an older parishioner asked him about using the rectory office for a meeting of the Ancient Order of Hibernians. And when he took a few more steps, a young man managed a few words with Father regarding the Baptism schedule for his newborn son. At long last Father John dodged his way to the kneeler where he whispered some quiet prayers for the departed man in the coffin. Wakes were always hard for him. What were the right words to say? Deep inside he knew there were no right words. Too bad he couldn't touch the man like Jesus did and watch him open his eyes and sit up. Wouldn't that be a great gift for the grieving wife and the young daughter!

Rising from the kneeler after waving the sign of the cross at the body, Father John kissed the little girl and embraced the young mother. He spoke of how sorry he was and asked some questions on when and how it all happened. But most of the time was spent in silence. The young widow was holding up very well and even managed a smile. Other people came by and as the young widow attended to them, Father John offered condolences to other family members, gave head nods to familiar faces, and even felt guilty that he didn't bring a miracle along. After a half hour of small talk that he didn't remember hearing or saying, he knelt for another prayer over the departed young father. How he hated wakes. How he wished he were Jesus. When he reached the street again, it was night.

Three teenage girls carrying video tapes came bopping down the street and teased him about being all dressed up in his black suit.

"They had better not be bad movies you have there. Let me see!" To his surprise, the girls handed him their plastic bag of tapes. He flipped through the titles, all horror films, and handed them back. "You'll be awake all night after looking at these spooky things."

As they walked along together back toward the church, two older high school girls called out from across the avenue.

"Hey, Father John," one of them shouted, "you're just the one I wanted to see. Wait up." The taller girl then danced between cars and crossed.

"What can I do for you?"

"I need a letter of recommendation. In order to get in the Honor Society at my high school, I need a letter from my parish priest. Will you write one for me?"

"Sure. What do I say?"

"Oh, just say all kinds of nice things about what a great kid I am. You know . . . " she laughed.

He leaned on the fender of a car and chatted for a few minutes with the happy teens. They spoke about their summer, their jobs, their school, and giggled between every sentence. They looked so young and so happy, yet they groaned about how old they were and wished they were younger.

"Okay! So when you have the letter written, just give me a call and I'll pick it up. Thanks a lot, Father. You're a doll." They leaned forward, giving him their ears to kiss, and waltzed away on the big sidewalk in front of the church.

Father John smiled. Imagine being called "a doll" by a young girl and "beautiful" by Tommy T-shirt all on the same night. He pushed off the fender and walked the last few steps to the rectory. That's when he saw "Raggedy Ann," the cursingest bag lady in all of Brooklyn. She stood at the bottom of the rectory stoop, loudly spewing a string of curses and foul language at the closed door. "You're all no good, you blankety blank Catholics" — these and other such epithets, neither repeatable nor printable, she flung at the empty stoop.

Not tonight, Father John muttered to himself. In order to get in he would have to brave the insults and verbal scourges of mindless Raggedy Ann. He tried to slip by her on the steps but she let him have it with one of her filthiest barrages. "You're a blankety blank!" she screamed in tones not sweet, but loud. The entire block would be awake if he didn't do something, so he turned around and pointed his finger at her.

"If you don't shut up and go away, I'm going to go in and call the police."

But that only made her louder and fouler. What a night, he thought, I bet the Mets are losing too. He towered above her and let her blast on until she exhausted both herself and her vocabulary. Then, as quickly as she started, she picked up her shopping bag and scurried down the street, muttering and cursing to herself into the night.

The four off-duty altar boys, who were sitting on the stoop across the street, watched the entire incident. Father John saw them and waved, but before he turned to put his key into the door, the tall altar boy called over to him.

"You should respect your elders, Father John."

And with his key in the door, he laughed long and loud and hard, and the kids laughed with him.

4

MICHAEL'S LAST SUMMER

Soon afterward he [Jesus] journeyed to a city called Nain, and his disciples and a large crowd accompanied him. As he drew near to the gate of the city, a man who had died was being carried out, the only son of his mother, and she was a widow. A large crowd from the city was with her. When the Lord saw her, he was moved with pity for her and said to her, "Do not weep." He stepped forward and touched the coffin; at this the bearers halted, and he said, "Young man, I tell you, arise!" The dead man sat up and began to speak, and Jesus gave him to his mother. Fear seized them all, and they glorified God, exclaiming, "A great prophet has arisen in our midst," and "God has visited his people." This report about him spread through the whole of Judea and in all the surrounding region (Luke 7:11-17).

Summer is for sunshine and swimming and slowing down. It's that happy, change-of-pace season for novel-reading in the backyard or stoop-sitting after supper. During June, July, and August there is to be no room in our lives for pressure or pain or tears. After all, summer is the sensational season, the time of warm and endless daylight, the yearly lull in our lives for leisure.

Subconsciously, Father John believed all this. Only good things happen in the summer, only splashing and laughing and singing. The cross, sickness, and especially death are for the December darkness, the January rains, the February snows — never for sunburnt summers.

Well, summer began that morning with the sun smiling from a gorgeous blue and cloudless Sunday sky. From backyards hidden by row houses, the green heads of lanky trees swayed above the rooftops. A gang of birds danced above the rectory bell tower and a sleepy auto slowly tiptoed down Sixtieth Street. It was June 1 — the unofficial beginning of summer.

Suddenly the phone's ring slashed through Father John's Sunday morning sleep-in. (He had been assigned to celebrate the noon Mass.) It made a jolting noise, a fearful sound like the voice of doom. Jumping out of the bed, Father John groped toward his desk and found the phone after its third ring.

"Hello," he muttered, half awake, into the receiver.

"John." It was Brother Tom in the rectory office. "There's a girl on the phone. She's the sister of your friend Michael. They just found him dead."

"Oh, no! Michael?" With those words Father John was awake and summer was over. "Put her through." A series of clicks led to the sound of tears and sniffles. "Father, this is Theresa. Michael died during the night. My mother went upstairs to wake him for nine o'clock Mass and found him dead." The voice broke down. "Father, could you please come over?"

And that's how Father John's summer started. With a shock. The wrong way. Summer, the season of life, began with death. Father John threw some water on his face and quickly dressed. Stopping downstairs he picked up the anointing oils of the Church and raced out the side door. People coming out of the 7:45 Mass must have sensed something was wrong because Father John raced past them and didn't even smile or nod or say hello. He reached Fifth Avenue and actually ran down the hill. One or two early beer tasters in the window of the corner bar and grill watched him blur by and scratched their heads. Something was up.

When he reached Michael's block, Father John had no doubt about what house to enter. Police cars, the ambulance, and the Bravo mobile double-parked halfway down the street. Neighbors, friends, and young people stood in silence on stoops and steps up and down the street. A policewoman held the door open as Father John raced by. "The top of the stairs, Father."

He jumped up the stairs, turned toward the hall room and froze in the doorway. There was Michael. The boy lay stretched across his bed, his eyes open in death. The summer sun, the sound of birds, the many shades of green filled the window frame above the head of the young man.

Father John's eyes watered. This was all wrong, he thought. "Old people are supposed to die like this — not this young man. Why, he's only twenty-one years old. His body is healthy and strong. He can't be dead. It's summer. It's Sunday. It's a day for the beach, not a day to die."

Father John touched the young man's forehead and felt the cold. Opening his holy oil container, he jabbed a thumb into the blessed oil and shakily marked a cross on the lad's forehead. What are the words? He couldn't remember them and, when he finally did, his tears got in the way. "If you are alive, we pray: through this holy anointing may the Lord in his love and mercy help you with the grace of the Holy Spirit. Amen." He was sobbing now because his young friend, Michael, was gone. Father John reached for the cold palms and signed them conditionally, too: "May the Lord who frees you from sin save you and raise you up. Amen." And summer was all over. . . .

Flipping through the green ritual, he found the commendation of the dying and began to say the prayers after death. His voice was muttering "Saints of God, come to his aid! Come to meet him, angels of the Lord!" But his mind was traveling back a couple of years to his first meeting with Michael.

"You see I go to Manhattan College where one of my courses is Religious Studies," the tall reddish-blond lad stood before him in the rectory office. "I have a term paper where I interview a priest on the Church, the world, and the priesthood. Could I interview you?"

"Sure," Father John smiled and led the lad into one of the parlors. The interview took an hour, tape recorder and all, like an untelevised Phil Donahue Show. Interviewer and interviewee both did very well. Months later, after one of the Sunday Masses, Michael stopped to talk to Father John at the back door of church.

"Really want to thank you, Father, for the interview. I wrote up the paper and got a B."

"You got a B? A lousy B?" Father John was teasing now. "All that work, all that time, and they give you a lousy B! When I get interviewed, I expect my interviewer to get an A." Both laughed and the formal acquaintance slowly softened into a friendship. Michael sent Father John a copy of the famous term paper. Then Christmas cards were exchanged. The months passed into years; they waved at each other in church and beeped each other when one spied the other from a car. Michael progressed from freshman all the way to junior before he needed another interview from Father John.

"May Christ, who called you, take you to himself; may angels lead you to Abraham's side" rolled from Father John's tongue while his thoughts ran to just a few weeks ago. This time Father John brought Michael inside the rectory to his office. "Wow! I ain't never been in here before," Michael took in the entire hallway.

"Spoken like a true college student," Father John remarked as he led him into his office. The tall, handsome young man sat on the couch while Father John eased into the rocker. It took Michael a while to get started; his eyes were roaming all over the office.

"I feel like I'm in the president's office," Michael teased back.

This time there was no tape recorder, not even a pad for notes. The priest and the collegian spoke about the Church's teaching on sexuality: Michael asking the questions, Father answering. The young man was looking forward to the end of exams and his twenty-first birthday.

"Just think," he said, "I'll be twenty-one and legal again for the second time." It was like two friends visiting each other. Michael spoke of his concern for his mother "who works too hard and does too much." He chided himself for his occasional inattention to his grandmother.

"My grandmother and I live on the top floor of the house. Sometimes I go up to my room and don't look in on her. Sometimes I take her for granted. I shouldn't do that."

As they chatted, Father John could sense that he was in the presence of a fine young man, a special person, a unique gift from God. It was going to be fun knowing him.

"Loving and merciful God, we entrust our brother to your mercy. You loved him greatly in this life; now that he is freed from all its cares, give him happiness and peace forever."

Father John was back to the present — with Michael and himself all alone in a room, only this time Father John's was the only voice to be heard.

Then Michael's grief-stricken mother burst into the room and threw herself across her son's body, pleading with him to come back. Father John wished he could say something, do something. Jesus once met a widowed mother at her only son's funeral procession outside of a town called Nain. He simply told the woman, "Do not weep." Jesus could say that because he was about to order the dead young man to rise. And the boy did. Why couldn't Father John do that now? Instead, all he could do was say to this sobbing mother: "Cry! Go ahead and cry!"

From then on everyone and everything was jumbled together. Michael's two sisters, neighbors, policemen and women, and so many others all passed in and out of his view, even Michael's grandmother, in her wheelchair, wondering what the fuss was. Someone had to tell the grandmother. "She knows something's up but she just thinks Michael is sick," Theresa said.

"Father, would you tell my mother?" Betty, Michael's mother, pleaded from behind her tears. So Father John walked into the front room and knelt before the old woman. "Hello, Grandma." He placed his hands over hers on the arms of the wheelchair.

"Oh, Father, I didn't know it was you back there. I thought you were a policeman. Isn't this terrible? Is Michael very sick, Father?"

"It's worse than that, Grandma."

The old woman looked him straight in the eyes. "What is it, Father? What do you mean?"

The only way to do this was to just come out and say it, so the priest took in a breath and said, "Grandma, Michael died in his sleep last night. Betty came upstairs to wake him and found him dead in the bed."

The old woman stared straight ahead. "Glory be to God," she said over and over half a dozen times. "Glory be to God. Poor Betty. How is she, Father?"

"Not too good but she'll be all right. How are you, Grandma?"

"I'll be fine, Father. Don't worry about me. I never cry." Her wrinkled hand went to her mouth.

And so began the long day of waiting, the day of the medical examiners, the day of the undertaker, the day of all those things and questions and words that have to do with death. It was a long, hot, dreadful day. The truth of it all kept coming back to the family after a moment of distraction and kept stabbing each of them like a crazed maniac jabbing a helpless victim who has already fallen to the ground. Phone calls. Doorbells. Neighbors. Arrangements. Food. The wake. The crowded Mass. All those young people crying in disbelief. The kind words. The entire block coming together. The burial. The long emptiness. . . .

Father John saw the grieving mother now and then and spent a lot of time thinking about Michael, about the uncertainty of life, about the sureness and finality of death. The boy was so young. He was so good. The Lord must have a reason for taking the good in the summer of life, he mused: the young and eternal Michael was now alive somewhere with God forever. It still wasn't summer though. Oh, there were plenty of hot days, there was a lot of sunshine; but to Father John, things still felt cold and sad and dark.

Then one day near the end of July a postcard came from Ireland. It was written by Michael's sister, Theresa.

"Hi, Father! I hope you're enjoying your summer. I'm having a great time at the University of Galway. I had a Mass said for Michael and am always lighting candles for him and Mom. They are in my thoughts and prayers always. I'd like to thank you for all you've done for my family. We truly needed your support at such a tragic time. I miss Michael very much and pray for courage and understanding. He was a great brother and a wonderful friend to me, and I do hope you are aware of how special you were to him. Thank you for everything. I'll stop by when I return at the end of the month.

Love,
Theresa."

Father John put the postcard down and smiled. It was summer once more. . . .

5

AN EMMAUS
STORY

Now that very day two of them [Jesus' followers] were going to
a village seven miles from Jerusalem called Emmaus, and they
were conversing about all the things that had occurred. And it
happened that while they were conversing and debating, Jesus
himself drew near and walked with them, but their eyes were
prevented from recognizing him. . . . One of them . . . said to
him . . . "Are you the only visitor to Jerusalem who does not
know of the things that have taken place there in these days?"
And he replied to them, "What sort of things?" They said to
him, "The things that happened to Jesus the Nazarene, who
was a prophet mighty in deed and word before God and all the
people, how our chief priests and rulers both handed him over
to a sentence of death and crucified him. . . . " And he said to
them, "Oh, how foolish you are! How slow of heart to believe
all that the prophets spoke! Was it not necessary that the
Messiah should suffer these things and enter into his glory?"
. . . But they urged him, "Stay with us. . . . " And it happened that, while he was with them at table, he took bread,
said the blessing, broke it, and gave it to them. . . . So they . . .
returned to Jerusalem . . . [and] recounted what had taken

place on the way and how he [Jesus] was made known to them in the breaking of the bread (Luke 24:13-16,18-20,25-26,29, 30,33,35).

Once upon a time there lived two boys who rolled around and grew up on the Brooklyn streets. The older boy could ballet with a basketball and Houdini with a hockey stick while the younger boy whiled away his after-school hours and double-featured his Saturdays and Sundays. The two of them lived three blocks apart but never really met until they found themselves five hundred miles away from the Brooklyn streets, in the same high school seminary classroom. They spent their next thirteen years as classmates, learning, laughing, singing, dancing, praying, playing, and dreaming together of becoming priests. The older lad, named Dan, and the younger lad, called Jack (in those early days), became the best of friends. Together their young lives made beautiful music and they invited many others to sing along. And then one golden Sunday morning they found themselves kneeling together on the same sanctuary floor under an anointing touch that made them priests forever. Soon they gave each other a final hug, laughed at a last joke, and hurried off separately to a heavy harvest.

"Now that very day two of them [Jesus' followers] were going to a village seven miles from Jerusalem called Emmaus, and they were conversing about all the things that had occurred. . . . "

Dan climbed the pulpits of the country. Standing atop mountainous marble, he spelled out in silver tones the splendor of God's love. He journeyed from New England villages to Hawaiian hotels, trying to make this a better world with words weaned from the Gospel and warmed in glorious colors from his rainbow imagination and set to the beautiful music of his manly and melodious voice.

Jack jogged back to the classrooms of his youth to teach other generations how to dream of and race toward the priesthood. And in the passing decades of years the two of them occasionally ran into each other, usually for an all too brief holiday hello or a quick lunch at a Bay Ridge restaurant. Both were happy. Both were doing well. Finally, after seventeen years, they found themselves in Brooklyn — together again! They would be living in the same rectory and ministering to the same people as parish priests. It looked like the perfect touch to a happy story, the Walt Disney twist in the tale of two friends.

"While they were conversing and debating, Jesus himself drew near and walked with them, but their eyes were prevented from recognizing him."

Then the disease came! Its black cloud locked itself in Dan's mind and threw away the key. Like the man seized by demons in the Gospel, Dan's body rattled and twisted in death-dealing convulsions. They finally carried him away strapped on a pallet and drove him to the priests' convalescent home. And to this day Dan rarely knows where he is. He passes day after monotonous day lost in some twilight zone. Somewhere between life and death, between fact and fantasy, between dreams and reality, Dan either sleeps or stares or remembers the long ago. On a terrible cross, he remains stretched out between heaven and earth.

And just a few weeks ago the two friends found themselves on the sanctuary floor once more concelebrating Mass. Only this time it was in the convalescent home for priests. Dozens of old and sickly priests in wheelchairs parked around the wooden altar table. And the younger friend was sitting next to his older classmate. Jack, in Lenten purple vestments, elbowed Dan who, draped in layers of afghans, was dozing away the Liturgy of the Word. Startled at first, Dan's chin slowly rose from his chest. Their eyes met and Dan smiled. Dan always smiled when he saw Jack's face.

So many faces and experiences remained buried in that black cloud in his mind, but Dan always recognized Jack.

The Mass continued and Jack spun off on a reverie of his own. Poor Dan, he thought. Here he is in his late forties, with a body like an old man's and a mind that can see back thirty years but can't remember yesterday. Yesterday. That was a good day. Yesterday Jack knelt at Dan's wheelchair in the dining room while the nurse fed him lunch. Jack called Dan the old nicknames, imitated the Irish brogue of Dan's father, tossed out the names of friends and classmates from thirty years back — and Dan laughed. His laugh sounded more like a hollow moan, not the manly, hearty laugh it used to be when he was well, but it was a laugh all the same.

"OK, Curley, let's have a test." For three decades Jack had been calling Dan "Curley" simply because he wasn't. "I'm going to ask you some questions and if you get the right answers, I'll take you to Coney Island." Dan's head lifted with a laugh. "First question: What year did we graduate from North East?"

"1956!" Dan smiled the right answer.

"Good! Now they get harder, so take your time. What year were we ordained?"

"1962!"

"Great! Say the secret word and win a thousand dollars." Jack Groucho Marxed Dan to more laughter. "Who directed our class play?"

"Me!" his papery voice weakly answered.

"And what was the name of it?"

"The Billion Dollar Saint!" Dan was happily on a roll.

"Who played the Billion Dollar Saint in the play?"

"The Mouse!" Dan responded with the nickname of another long-ago priest friend.

"Nurse, there's absolutely nothing wrong with this man. He's obviously got it made up here, sitting around all day with gorgeous nurses feeding him.'' Jack's routine, this time in a German accent, had both Dan and the nurse breaking up.

"He hasn't laughed like this in months," the nurse said. "You're just what the doctor ordered."

Just what the doctor ordered! Jack wished with all his heart that he could somehow reach in and unlock that black cloud and bring Dan back to health. Dan always knew the answers of long ago but now he couldn't tell you what day of the week or what month of the year it was.

Jack pushed Dan in his wheelchair back to his room, chattering the length of the corridor about anything that would make Dan smile, while secretly praying that God would cure his clouded brain and weakened body. "Are you the only visitor to Jerusalem who does not know of the things that have taken place there in these days?"

With Dan tucked under many colored afghans in his hospital bed, Jack leaned over the bed's guardrails. They quietly looked at each other.

"What happened to me?" Now it was Dan's turn to ask Jack the hard questions and, once more, Jack told him about the January day five years ago when the sickness attacked him in the Brooklyn rectory.

"But I was never stationed in Brooklyn," Dan confusedly protested.

"You were, Dan. We were together."

"Are you stationed in Brooklyn?"

"Yeah, I've been there since 1980. We were together."

"Really?" Dan's eyes looked away. "I wish I could remember . . . I wish I could get well and get out of here. . . . ''

Silence. The words from the Emmaus story sounded in Jack's heart: how Jesus had been handed over to a sentence of death by the chief priests and rulers.

The words of the Our Father at the concelebrated Mass brought

Jack back to the present. He was now standing while his friend slumped in a semi-doze in the wheelchair next to him. And Jack prayed these words for Dan. The celebrant continued, "Deliver us, Lord, from every evil and grant us peace in our day. In your mercy keep us free from sin and protect us from all anxiety. . . . " That's when the words from the Emmaus story boomed and echoed in his heart and found their way into his soul. "How foolish you are! How slow of heart to believe all that the prophets spoke! Was it not necessary that the Messiah should suffer these things and enter into his glory?" Jack smiled inside and said "Yes" for himself and "Yes" for Dan.

The celebrant passed the plate of broken bread to Jack to distribute to the sick and aged priests. He turned toward Dan, took the Body of Christ and handed it to him. Their eyes met again and Dan smiled. " . . . the two recounted what had taken place on the way and how he was made known to them in the breaking of the bread."

6

THE DAYS OF
WINE AND ALDO

[The mother of Jesus] said to the servers, "Do whatever he tells you." Now there were six stone water jars there for Jewish ceremonial washings, each holding twenty to thirty gallons. Jesus told them, "Fill the jars with water." So they filled them to the brim. Then he told them, "Draw some out now and take it to the headwaiter." So they took it. And when the headwaiter tasted the water that had become wine, without knowing where it came from (although the servers who had drawn the water knew), the headwaiter called the bridegroom and said to him, "Everyone serves good wine first, and then when people have drunk freely, an inferior one; but you have kept the good wine until now" (John 2:5-10).

Father John met Aldo only twice in their lifetime. The first visit lasted about forty minutes, but in that short time they became friends for life. And after their talk together, Aldo handed Father John a bottle of wine. A week later the priest encountered Aldo again and once more there was the wine; only this time it was in a glass cruet; this time it was his granddaughter who handed it to him; this time it was his funeral Mass where they became friends for eternity.

But that's the *end* of the story. Let's go back to the beginning of the days of wine and Aldo. It was a hectic afternoon in late September when Rose from the front office stood in Father John's doorway with a phone message in her hand. "A man from the parish, sick with cancer, his wife called, would like a priest, no hurry, come when you can, bring the holy oils and the Eucharist, don't tell him you have them, just drop in sometime, let him ask for the sacraments."

Father John took the message and saw the name for the first time — Aldo. The wine commercial with the little man in the white suit and white fedora strutting through a sidewalk cafe chased by a bevy of beauties crying out "Aldo! Aldo!" immediately fermented in his memory. Never really met a man named "Aldo" before, he mused. The name itself spoke of wine and sent the sounds of wine bubbling through his brain: all the famous brand names. The priest smiled and stuffed the message into his shirt pocket. Better go to him now. Tomorrow might be even more hectic and I might forget and then Aldo would slip into oblivion.

It was a cold, steel-gray afternoon, more like late November than September, when Father John parked on a nearby street and headed into the apartment house where Aldo lived. The buzzer at the foyer door welcomed him and he slowly walked up the stairs. His pockets bulged with ritual book, holy water, containers for the Eucharist and anointing oils, and his stole — Aldo's wife did not want her husband alarmed at the sight of all the Church's sacramental tools and instruments of emergency. A smiling woman met him at the door.

"Oh, hello, Father. Didn't expect you so soon."

She led Father John through the hallway to the living room where, seated in a comfortable recliner, wearing his pajamas, sat his soon-to-be friend, Aldo. He was a big man in his mid sixties with a rather friendly but frightened face. Both his wife and his sister had been sitting there talking with him, but as soon as introductions were completed they rose with the usual "We'll leave you two alone" and disappeared down the hallway into the small kitchen.

Father John sat on the footstool right in front of Aldo. He looked healthy. Had he not been in his pajamas, the priest would never have taken the man to be sick. His story sounded like so many others: a year and a half of operations, tumors, chemotherapy, hospitals, doctors. A lonely tear welled in his eye and sadly sparkled at the priest.

"I'm very afraid, Father," he said.

Father John leaned over and touched the hand that gripped his knee. "Is there much pain?"

"No! It's not that. I just get weak. Sometimes I can't remember things. And now I'm scared."

"Would you like confession and absolution, Aldo?"

"You can do it here?"

"Sure."

"Good. I'd like that." So Aldo made his confession and Father John said some words and rested his hand on the tumor-filled skull as he absolved him. That's when Aldo smiled. It was a beautiful, warm, and manly smile. He was feeling better already.

Sensing the time was ripe, Father John popped the question. "Aldo, would you like to receive the Sacrament of the Sick — the anointing?"

"Here?" He looked surprised. "Now?"

"Yeah, I have the oils with me." He pulled the holy oil container and ritual book from his pocket.

"Sure," he answered, " . . . if it's OK."

"Believe me. It's OK. I can even give you Communion after I anoint you."

"You got Communion with you too?"

Father John pulled the container with the white host from his other pocket. Aldo smiled again. "You certainly come prepared. What else you got in those pockets?"

"Just holy water." Out came the plastic bottle of holy water. He placed the sacrament and all the sacramentals on the end table at Aldo's elbow and called to the two women in the kitchen. "Ladies, would you like to join us?"

The two women came into the living room and sat in a semicircle around Aldo. The familiar holy words seemed to transform the people there into a happy, peaceful gathering. "Through this holy anointing, may the Lord in his love and mercy help you with the grace of the Holy Spirit. Amen." Father John traced a cross of oil on Aldo's diseased forehead. Finally he stood before him holding the tiny white sacrament in his fingers. "This is the Lamb of God who takes away the sins of the world. Happy are those . . . " Aldo opened his mouth and Father John placed the Lord on his tongue.

When the sacraments were over, the four of them sat for a chat. Aldo's wife and his sister were obviously happy with the visit but a glimmer of concern suddenly shadowed Aldo's expression.

"Anything wrong?" the priest asked.

"Yeah. There's one thing I never mentioned to you. I never got Confirmation. When I was a kid, I was stubborn and didn't make my Confirmation. Is that a problem?"

"No problem, Aldo," Father John smiled. "You want Confirmation? I'll give it to you."

"Don't tell me you got that in your pocket, too?" They all laughed.

"No! We can make a date next week sometime or whenever. And I can come over and confirm you. OK?"

"But can *you* confirm, Father?" His sister was giving a Canon Law test.

"Sure. In this case, I can. It's an emergency." Smiles came with the answer and Father John continued. "I'll give you a call next week and we can set a date."

"That'd be nice." For the first time, Aldo sat all the way back in his recliner. He looked relieved, less afraid. "Tell me, Father, do you like Italian food?"

"Love it!" Father John answered.

"Good!" He turned toward his wife. "Get Father a bottle of my favorite wine. He can have it with his next Italian meal." Aldo's wife raced into the hallway and soon returned holding a bottle of fine red wine. She handed it to Aldo who took it in both hands and then leaned forward for the presentation. "This is for you, Father, my friend. Enjoy it and thank you."

It was a beautiful gift. Never before had Father John received a bottle of wine at a sick call. A tremendous smile creased Aldo's face as he handed Father the bottle. "Thanks a lot. I'll look in on you again next week. Don't be afraid. We're not going to leave you alone." Father John shook his hand, said the customary good-byes, and walked to the car with Aldo's wine cradled in his arm.

That was Thursday. Aldo died on Sunday. Father John went to the wake on Tuesday and celebrated the funeral Mass on Wednesday. And he never missed his forty-minute friend as much as he did when his granddaughter handed him the cruet of wine at the Offertory procession. Another gift of wine from Aldo, a gift for the Eucharistic meal, a gift that he raised in a silver chalice, in a holy toast to his friend and his Lord.

Aldo's bottle of red wine still stands as a friendly presence on the file cabinet in Father John's office. He is saving it for an Italian meal when he can raise the glass and offer another toast to the days of wine and his friend, Aldo.

7

CHARLIE'S PROMISE

Now there was a Pharisee named Nicodemus, a ruler of the Jews. He came to Jesus at night and said to him, "Rabbi, we know that you are a teacher who has come from God, for no one can do these signs that you are doing unless God is with him." Jesus answered and said to him, "Amen, amen, I say to you, no one can see the kingdom of God without being born from above." Nicodemus said to him, "How can a person once grown old be born again? Surely he cannot reenter his mother's womb and be born again, can he?" Jesus answered, "Amen, amen, I say to you, no one can enter the kingdom of God without being born of water and Spirit. What is born of flesh is flesh and what is born of spirit is spirit. . . . ' " Nicodemus answered and said to him, "How can this happen?" Jesus answered and said to him, "You are the teacher of Israel and you do not understand this? Amen, amen, I say to you, we speak of what we know and we testify to what we have seen, but you people do not accept our testimony. If I tell you about earthly things and you do not believe, how will you believe if I tell you about heavenly things? No one has gone up to heaven except the one who has come down from heaven, the Son of Man (John 3:1-6,9-13).

The above Gospel scene paints a rather serious and somber scene of a certain senior citizen Pharisee named Nicodemus. In the black of night, on the QT, and wrapped in layers of disguising robes, he slithered into Jesus' apartment to ask the immortal question: "How can a man be born again when he is old?"

It wasn't that way with Charlie, the retired insurance man. One wintry afternoon while on his way home from a Fifth Avenue store, Charlie recalled a promise he had made long ago to his wife. "Someday before I die," he told her, "I'll become a Catholic." Those words, uttered casually to his wife, seemed to jab him as he walked up Fifty-Ninth Street, past the immense gray stone church. It was only a promise spoken so long ago, probably at the kitchen table, scrambled between weekday supper conversation, said halfheartedly with the sincerity of most New Year's resolutions. But ever since the night she told him she wasn't feeling well and left him watching "Family Feud" on TV to lay down on her bed and die, the promise became a haunting. "Someday before I die, I'll become a Catholic."

And sometimes, from somewhere out of the beyond, Charlie thought he could hear her ask him, "When, Charlie, when?" He would roll over before sleep and resolve to drop into the rectory and speak to a priest about it. But he never did and so the promise continued to haunt him.

It was then that he stopped walking — right at the foot of the rectory steps. He looked up at the large wooden door, framed with stained glass. I have no idea how to even go about this, he thought. Does one just go in there and tell whoever is at the office window to make him a Catholic? There's probably a ton of studying to do. How can a seventy-one year old widower go back to school again? How can a man be born again once he is old? Charlie gave a what-have-I-got-to-lose shrug and slowly walked up the rectory steps. And, unlike Nicodemus who sneaked to Jesus under the blanket of night, Charlie came searching for the Lord in broad winter's daylight, with the body of an old man and the simplicity of a child — a child who believed in keeping promises.

Everything then happened very fast for Charlie. A smiling Brother pointed him to a seat while he rang for Father John. The priest listened to the story of Charlie's promise and invited him to join the parish's Adult Inquiry class, where he could learn more about the Catholic faith. "I'm not so hot with books, Father. Haven't been to school in years. Don't even know if I'll pass the tests," Charlie informed the priest.

"There are *no* tests, Charlie. Relax! You don't have to be a scholar to become a Catholic. It's got more to do with faith than knowledge." Father John calmed Charlie so much that, for the first time all afternoon, a smile underlined the old man's white, pencil-line mustache.

So on the following Tuesday evening, like a child on his first day of school, Charlie timidly walked into a classroom in the basement of the high school. Several other adults were already chatting in friendly groups.

"Good evening, everyone," Father John began. "I'd like you to welcome Charlie to our class tonight. He'll be with us each week. He's interested in becoming a Catholic." Smiling faces and clapping hands made Charlie blush. "Hi, Charlie!" "Hello, Charlie!" "Welcome, Charlie!" His head nodded up and down to each smiling face. The journey began and Charlie was keeping his promise.

It was a truly happy year for Charlie. Each week Father handed out books, pamphlets, typed pages, even New Testaments. And Charlie diligently took notes. Whenever the priest's words lost him, Charlie would cry out: "I'm not getting this. There's so much. What's that word again? Eucharist? How am I going to spell it? I can't even remember it."

But bits and pieces of beliefs began to seep through to Charlie and he returned each Tuesday night with his personal briefcase. He copied every word he could that came from Father's mouth; he wrote out definitions and diagrams from the blackboard; he read all the handouts and each week when he got home he rewrote his scribbled jottings neatly into his notebook.

And all the while Charlie was experiencing community. No longer a class full of strangers, the group had become a room full of friends. Charlie found a family once more. There was Patricia, "the Chinese goil who was getting the woiks" (that's Baptism, Confirmation, First Communion, and Matrimony); there was Tony, "the Greek feller with the family, who's my buddy"; there was Jose, "the young Spanish guy Father teased a lot"; and Luis, "the poor guy who always came in late for classes."

In no time at all, it was Charlie who would walk into the classroom and greet every individual by name. He even welcomed the new people, making them feel immediately at home. Without a vote being taken, Charlie became the spokesperson of the class, the official welcomer, the quasi-father of a family, fostered by faith. His smiling mustache in the back row became a necessary ingredient of each week's session while a wrinkled question mark on his forehead became an indicator to the priest that he was teaching over everyone's head.

"I see by Charlie's face that you guys aren't understanding a thing I'm saying." Father John would pause.

"Oh, no, it's not that, Father," Charlie would speak up. "I realize that you have to teach this sacrament stuff. But when are you going to get to the important stuff?"

"Like what, Charlie?"

"Like when do we sit and when do we stand and when do we kneel in church?"

"That's not all that important, Charlie."

"Maybe not for you. But I don't want everyone laughing at me when I'm sitting and I'm supposed to be standing." Charlie, always the practical man, knew how to get to the heart of things.

And one night after class as the people were saying their good-nights before starting for home, Charlie approached Father in the front of the room. "Father, just when am I gonna make the big step?"

"Won't be long now, Charlie. It won't be long."

"Well, it better be soon. I'm ready and I made up my mind to become a Catholic. But we don't have too much time left. I was to the doctor this week and he said my ticker was bad. I may have only about six months to live and I want to keep my promise. I don't have much time and neither do you. So you better hurry."

The weeks piled on, one after the other, and Charlie, along with his faith friends, inched closer and closer to what they called "the big event" — their reception into the Catholic Church. And on the first Sunday of Lent at a crowded Mass, the parishioners watched Charlie and his friends sign a document called "The Petition of Election" and Charlie was now one of the elect. The class then traveled to the cathedral one night and Charlie shook hands with the bishop himself. "He called me 'Charlie.' Wasn't that nice!"

And finally after over a year of preparation, Charlie and his friends gathered around the altar platform in the lower church during the Easter Vigil. Charlie thrice professed his belief in God — the Father and the Son and the Holy Spirit — with a loud "I do." And he renounced sin and evil and Satan with an even louder "I do" each time. He was then signed on the forehead with the Oil of Chrism as a confirmed Catholic Christian with the name "Joseph." And with hundreds of lifetime Catholics, Charlie came forward for his very first Holy Communion in seventy-one years. And the community of believers gave him a cheerful applause and a happy welcome. And one soul, a beloved wife, applauded her husband from the halls of heaven because she still loved him and also because he had kept his promise.

8

MEGHAN!

And people were bringing children to him that he might touch them, but the disciples rebuked them. When Jesus saw this he became indignant and said to them, ''Let the children come to me; do not prevent them, for the kingdom of God belongs to such as these. Amen, I say to you, whoever does not accept the kingdom of God like a child will not enter it.'' Then he embraced them and blessed them, placing his hands on them. (Mark 10:13-16).

Hi, everyone! I'm not one of your biggest parishioners. You see, I was just born and weigh only a few pounds and measure a matter of inches. Just a few weeks ago at my Baptism, I officially became a member of your parish and also a real live sister to all of you. I was only thirty days old when my mother and father bundled me in a womb of whiteness one rainy Sunday afternoon and took me up to your church (ours now) for my very first time. I guess the cold fresh air tired me out 'cause I don't remember much about the Baptism ceremony. I fell asleep — again.

I remember being passed around quite a bit. My father's thumb tickled me as he traced the cross on my forehead. His happiness must have traveled right through his body, into his thumb, and onto my little head. It felt real good. My mother passed me to my big sister who held me while this other man ("Father John" everyone called him), all dressed in white, turned on a waterfall of life and it rolled all over my head and into a silver tub beneath me. I opened my eyes and all I could see were their funny faces of love. They all looked so happy. When they finished all their words and motions, a lot of clapping woke me. I sleep quite a lot. My mother told someone the other day that I don't have my nights and days figured out yet. I wonder what she means.

Well anyway, after all the clapping, many more funny faces appeared above me just to look at me. Some even wanted to hold me. So I was passed around again. Everybody seems to like me. I wonder why; I just got here. But it sure is a nice feeling. I'm glad I came and everybody I've met so far seems to be glad I'm here too. You people certainly have a way of making a girl feel right at home.

The next time I woke up I was lying in my bassinet in some big hall. Nice lights hung from the ceiling, but face after smiling face kept hovering above me. The faces "oohed" and "aahed" at me and some even spoke things like "Isn't she adorable?" I wonder what's "adorable." As I told you, I don't know too much; I just got here. The one thing I do know is that I'm very small. Everyone else is way bigger than I am. In fact, it's a tremendously big world you have here. In my thirty days so far, I haven't met anyone my size. I suppose I will though. I hope so.

The hall was a really noisy place. All kinds of faces kept touching my parents' faces with theirs. Other faces jumped around together in the middle of the hall to the "ay-dee-die-dee" sounds of two guys on a platform at the other end of this big room. On either side of me the faces placed big ribboned boxes in pretty colors. Wonder what's in those boxes? I got the feeling that everyone was happy. And it seemed to be because of me. I'm getting sleepy again. I'll be back.

We all seemed to have been in this hall a long time. I opened my eyes again and saw my mother putting one of those white things around my middle. She does that a lot. It's very comfortable in this world and the service is terrific. I'm always warm and whenever I get this strange feeling of emptiness, my mother feeds me. All I have to do is open my mouth and scream, and a bunch of faces come running to me. They pick me up, make strange sounds, and in no time give me something to eat. Very welcoming people in this world!

I don't have too much to tell you since I only just got here. But I like it very much so far. I live in this house with four other and bigger faces. They are always smiling at me. One face is my father. So often when it's dark and I'm awake, I'll open my mouth and make a loud noise. He comes through the darkness and picks me up to rock me in his big arms. He says all kinds of nice things to me. I don't know what they are yet but I guess I'll find out soon enough. I like it when he puts his gigantic finger on my chin and makes a funny sound. I'm so glad he's my father. It feels so good in his arms. That must be love. I hear that word a lot. Can't tell you what anything means. Remember I can't even talk yet.

The other face is my mother. She sings and hums so many nice sounds at me. I don't know who's happier, my mother or my father. They both seem to like me very much. I don't have those pains in my middle as long as my mother is around. All I have to do is open my mouth and she presses me close to her to feed me. She's so warm and happy. I wonder if there are other people in this world who have mothers and fathers like I do. I think I'm very lucky.

The other two faces in our house are my sister and brother. They are both very old. They are big too, like my mother and father. They held me when I went to your church (I mean, ''our church'') for the Baptism so I guess they're more than just brother and sister to me. They had a big part to play in that ceremony. Must ask them about it when I learn to talk. I don't know how I'll ever get to do that though. Talking seems so hard. Must listen more to the sounds they make and imitate them. But all they do is imitate me. I want to imitate them. They seem like such nice people to imitate. Oops! I'm getting tired again. I'll talk to you when I wake up.

It's a nice house we all live in. I hear lots of laughter. And whenever people come home from what they call "work," they run upstairs to see me, make noises at me or hold me. My father comes home with little things for me. He held a little gold circle before my face one day and said something that sounded like "bracelet." I have no idea what it's for, but I know it's for me and I know it makes him happy. He makes me happy too. I just love his face. It's always bright, almost shining.

Anytime those happy, smiling faces loom over me, they make the sound "Meghan." My sister and brother use that sound a lot too. I think it means me because at my Baptism, when the man in white waterfalled me, I heard sounds like "Meghan," "Father," "Son," and "Spirit." I hope it's my name.

Well, this time I'm getting hungry so I have to go. Since that day they brought me to church, I'm getting the feeling that my family is bigger than the four people I live with. You have all been so nice to me that I feel that you must be brothers and sisters to me too. If that's true, then keep an eye on me as I grow. Your welcoming love has been really swell. Each day is an adventure. In a way I can't wait to hear about the One who started all of this.

I'm so glad to be alive, to be here and have the mother and the father and the brother and the sister I have. And I'm just as thrilled that all of you are in some wonderful and mysterious way my brothers and sisters also. Gosh, don't we have a big and happy family? Hope to see you lots more in the days ahead.

It's time to yell for some food. See you soon. As they say a lot in my house, "I love you!"

9

WORDS OF WISDOM
FROM JOE
THE ENGRAVER

[Jesus said:] "You are the salt of the earth. But if salt loses its taste, with what can it be seasoned? It is no longer good for anything but to be thrown out and trampled underfoot. You are the light of the world. A city set on a mountain cannot be hidden. Nor do they light a lamp and then put it under a bushel basket; it is set on a lampstand, where it gives light to all in the house. Just so, your light must shine before others, that they may see your good deeds and glorify your heavenly Father" (Matthew 5:13-16).

The Word of God once said that as long as heaven and earth last, not the smallest letter, not the smallest part of a letter of the Law will be done away with. And wasn't it his Father who promised to write his law on our hearts? Well, the other day Father John met a man named Joe who not only makes a living on words but who reminded him of *the Word*. No, he's not a famous author who gives birth to books. Joe's an engraver with cuts and callouses on his hard hands and stubble on his gray chin. He wears green work pants and shirt around his wiry body, passing each workday digging letters and words onto small metal plates. Believe it or not, many of Joe's words endure at this moment in many homes. They are engraved on thousands of trophies and plaques that stand on tops of dining room china closets or rest in the darkness of brownstone cellars or sleep on bottoms of old trunks or among blankets of dust under many a bed.

Trophies and awards have a knack of increasing and multiplying, growing invisible amidst all our household clutter. But Joe's words remain, carved in metal, not stone. What he has written, he has written. Some of his greatest hits are: "Fourth Place, Junior Division, 68th Precinct Bowling League" or the popular "M.V.P., O.L.P.H. Soccer League." The amazing thing, however, about Joe the Engraver is that the words he cuts with his lips, teeth, and tongue will endure longer than the words he rubs into hard metal with his engraving machine.

One afternoon Father John squeezed into Joe's shop to get some engraving done. His shop is the size of a rectory parlor, yet there's hardly room for two people at the same time. Boxes, workbench, trophies, sheets of metal, orders, bills, catalogs, deliveries of varied shapes and sizes turn Joe's shop into a complete mess. Joe was in the corner at his machine.

"Joe, I need three small plates engraved to put on these lectionaries as memorials." Father John handed him a penciled order. "Can you do it?"

"Can I do it?" Joe was quasi-insulted. "Of course I can do it."

"Great. When should I come back and pick them up?"

"I'll get rid of you now. Sit down." He pointed Father John to a tall stool and his hands pulled letters from his alphabet tray faster than a magician could pull rabbits from a top hat. The words "in memory of" appeared on his machine before Father John's bottom

found the stool. The priest half-stood and watched him trace —
with a large stylus in one hand — big letters from his alphabet tray,
while guiding a smaller nail-like pen onto a small gold plate with
the other hand.

"So that's how you do it? You trace on a machine." Father John
feigned shock. "For years I thought you guys, like Michelangelo,
chiseled each letter on each trophy by hand."

"That's how I started and earned enough money to buy this
machine." Joe stabbed Father John with his white eyes. "Sit
down!"

The priest disobeyed and stood behind him to witness his magic.
"I don't like people watching me when I work," Joe said. "Even
though I'm a good engraver, I'm a lousy speller." He turned and
laughed.

"Really?"

"Sure! See my dictionary!" Joe pointed to a wall and bookcase
in front of him. Thousands of words and phrases like "Our Lady of
Guadalupe" and "Czestochowa" and "Assisi," "Ephraim" and
even "Perpetual Help" were scratched there in pencil. "Whenever
I engrave a word with a tricky spelling, I put it in my dictionary —
the wall. If I ever move from this store, the wall's gotta come with
me."

Joe's hands were quicker than Father's eyes, but the words he
spoke were deeper and sharper than the ones he engraved. Suddenly the day's FM music from his radio stopped for a credit card
commercial. "Don't leave home without it." That's when Joe
stopped his magic and scowled at the radio, "Don't leave home
without it, my foot! They won't let me leave home *with* it."

Then, with a wisdom gleaned from the streets and the years, Joe
began to engrave a verbal trophy. "Father, I have a good business
here. See these bills? Pay 'em all with cash. And I got some money
in the bank. See!" His left hand pulled a few worn bank books
from one pocket; his right drew a rubber-banded wad of bills from

the other. "Yet those creeps won't give me a lousy credit card 'cause I don't owe nobody no money."

Joe was on a roll. "There's too many people these days that worry about money. This guy I know, he's retired. All day long he figures ways to get more interest on the money he loans. His mind's goin' like a computer. For what? Every wakin' minute is about the buck. Some retirement! Ha! He's so worried about how he can get more that it's gonna kill him."

Joe's choice of words were Brooklyn vintage, but as he fired away, gesturing with the metal plate he held in his hand, his thoughts were a carpenter's from long ago telling a hillside crowd, "Do not store up for yourselves treasures on earth, where moth and decay destroy . . . " (Matthew 6:19).

"I enjoy my work. I raised my family and once in a while me and my wife go to Atlantic City for a dinner and a show." He was putting tape to the back of the engraved plate, all the while looking at Father John. "I got this son who goes to Tiffany's to buy a gold necklace for his wife. Don't get me wrong, she's a great daughter-in-law. 'Look at this necklace I got her,' he says. 'Got a great deal, only one hundred fifty bucks.' Father, she'll wear it once or twice a year and then leave it in some box on her dresser. Life is to be lived one day at a time, not to pile up stuff."

"For where your treasure is, there also will your heart be" (Matthew 6:21).

Joe the engraver took a deep breath and leaned closer. "This society tells me I'm supposed to leave thousands of dollars to my kids. Who says? One son will take the money and buy a Caddy, another will buy a boat. Look out that window — next to the curb. I drive around in a '69 Ford. So I'm supposed to leave a fortune so they can drive or sail around in luxury while I'm in the ground eating dirt? Baloney! I worked all my life. Let them work too."

Joe's words were coming fast and Father John was smiling, probably because the priest was hearing "Look at the birds in the sky; they do not sow or reap, they gather nothing into barns, yet your heavenly Father feeds them'' (Matthew 6:26). Joe was a free person, a hardworking man, a man with a spirituality akin to another laborer of long ago but he never realized it. His words etched out phrases on Divine Providence with such sharp clarity that Father John could hear Jesus talking about birds of the air and every hair on your head being counted and why worry about tomorrow.

While the minutes passed, the priest's ears tasted each new morsel that came from the engraver, delivering his words of wisdom. ''Next week my wife and me are married thirty-five years. If I can get away from all this work, maybe the both of us will take three days off and go to Atlantic City. We enjoy it. She's a good lady.''

Father John sat there enthralled for an hour and would be there still had not Joe the engraver finished putting the gold ''in memory of'' plates on the three lectionaries.

''Here,'' he said. ''All done!''

The trance from Joe's magic fingers and God-spelling words over, Father John reached for his wallet.

''What'll that be, Joe?''

''Forget it,'' he pushed the wallet away.

''Joe, this money was donated to me to pay for the engraving. Please let me pay you.'' Father John would have gotten a better response from his wall of words.

''Put it in the collection!'' He was straightening bills and business envelopes on his workbench.

''Joe, your anniversary's next week. Why not use this for vacation money?''

He laughed. ''Listen. That wouldn't take me very far. It ain't worth it. Put it in the collection. I'm a Catholic but I still need all the help I can get. Give it to the church.''

''Thanks, Joe! You're kind and your work is beautiful.''

"I know I'm no Michelangelo but I'm pretty good at engraving words."

"You're also pretty good at speaking words."

"Get outta here!" Joe was obviously embarrassed. After the two shook hands, Father John wormed his way out of the shop. On the street it struck him that he just had an experience with "the salt of the earth and the light of the world." Every once in a while we have the experience of meeting a person who's a treasure. Joe the Engraver was such a treasure. He made Father John smile; he made him think. "Do not worry and say 'What are we to eat?' or 'What are we to drink?' or 'What are we to wear?' " and "Seek first the kingdom [of God] and his righteousness, and all these things will be given you besides" (Matthew 6:31,33) — these and other words of a table and chair maker from years back matched the words of a letter and word maker of today.

Father John wasn't present when Jesus spoke of "the salt of the earth and the light of the world," but he is glad that he didn't miss these words of wisdom from Joe the Engraver.

10
LOUIS

Then he [Jesus] sat down, called the Twelve, and said to them, "If anyone wishes to be first, he shall be the last of all and the servant of all." Taking a child he placed it in their midst, and putting his arms around it he said to them, "Whoever receives one child such as this in my name, receives me; and whoever receives me, receives not me but the One who sent me" (Mark 9:35-37).

The main event of his week is attending the 11:30 Sunday Eucharist. He is usually there fifteen minutes ahead of time, sitting on the edge of his seat in the first or second row of the Fifty-Ninth Street alcove. His unzipped winter coat reveals a colorful woolen sweater. Chubby fingers play with the missalette and anxious eyes dart about the altar platform, hoping to spy his friends in the choir. As the 11:30 alcove people start arriving, his head turns this way and that to greet the familiar faces with his trademark smile or a wave or even a few words of conversation. If he talks too much or too loudly, his mother, to his right, puts her hand on his knee to calm him, while his father, to his left, quietly inches closer to him.

He has become the celebrity of the 11:30 celebrants and is such a happy person that his contagious joy and sense of well-being touch all who gather in the Fifty-Ninth Street alcove for the 11:30 Eucharist. He is only thirteen years old and his name is Louis.

No sooner does Louis settle down than the big priest appears on the sanctuary platform, checking the missal or adjusting the microphone. Louis spots the priest and bubbles over with so much excitement that he shouts out, "Hey, Jaaa. . . . "

The priest looks over, instantly smiles, stops what he is doing, and walks over for his Sunday visit with Louis.

"Hey, Louie! How's the kid?"

"Hey, Jaaa. . . . " Louis stretches out his arm and the two friends shake fingers.

"Louis, his name is Father. Call him Father, not Jack." His mother is embarrassed.

"Hey, Faaa. . . . " Louis' eyes glisten as they climb up the priest's black shirt to the face high above him.

"Where are you going today, Louie?" The priest always asks the same question, knowing that he will get the same answer.

"Groundroun!" The chubby hands come together in a clap of anxious anticipation. Louis' pleasures in life are quite simple: Sunday brunch at the "Ground Round" in the Staten Island Mall or a hamburger at "McDonald's" after Mass. Some Sundays Louis will tell the priest that he is going to the "airplaneport," and his mother will quickly add, "That's 'airport,' Louis. Not airplaneport." Other weeks he will burst with the good news that he is going home for "sketti balls" and his mother will whisper "spaghetti with meatballs" to the priest, who isn't smart enough to catch many of Louis' expressions.

Their conversation usually concludes as Louis catches sight of the choir setting up their chairs. Another big priest in an alb, carrying a music stand, comes out of the sacristy and Louis, once again, shouts his Sunday greeting, "Hey, Steeeee. . . . "

His mother blushes once more and gently reminds him, "Louis, his name is Father. Call him Father, not Steve."

The Mass begins and Louis stands and sings along with everyone else. He sometimes extends his arms out in imitation of the celebrant during the Eucharistic Prayer. And when the priest and ministers leave the altar during the recessional hymn, Louis invariably claps his hands in a way that shouts to the assembly that they have all done their tasks well. This short and stout boy-child, who has trouble speaking, suddenly becomes the eloquent affirmer of the 11:30 worshiping people. His clapping hands have a way of transforming a faceless crowd into a smiling community.

Louis' Sunday becomes complete when the big priest occasionally invites him to present the ciborium with the hosts and the cruets with the wine and water at the Offertory procession. The thrill of his Christmas occurred at the Midnight Mass, when he and his parents came all the way from the back of the church and handed the gifts to the pastor. That even pushed Santa Claus out of the spotlight. Louis loves to participate in every way he can during our Sunday liturgies and, in his own simple, beautiful, childlike way, he reminds the rest of us of the joy there is in our coming together.

Each weekday morning at eight o'clock, Louis slowly struggles up the steps of a school bus that brings him to P.S. 226 for his classes in special education. He puts in a long day, arriving home again at 3:30 in the afternoon. After school, he plays with his cats or his three Dobermans or walks with his mother to the delicatessen on Fifth Avenue. The short trip to the store usually takes longer for Louis than for the others because he stops to chat with all his friends and neighbors on the street. After supper, Louis tackles his home computer which he can handle with the best of the experts.

Each month on first Friday evenings, Louis and his mother attend the Healing Mass in the lower church at 7:30 p.m. After the Mass one night, the visiting Carmelite priest invited all the participants to come up to the sanctuary where he would pray over each person individually. Hand in hand, Louis and his mother joined the long line. The priest extended his hands and silently prayed over Louis' mother. Then leaning down, he asked Louis what he would like most of all from God. Louis looked up, smiled, and without a moment's hesitation blurted out "Coke and pizza!" The entire line of praying people popped with the laughter of healing. The priest bent over and embraced the gift of Louis. And the Lord healed many a heart that night with the simple, honest answer of one of his special children.

The 11:30 Mass ended and the church slowly emptied. An old woman in widow's black knelt all alone in the back of the church. Her eyes were closed and her lips raced rapidly in cross-laden prayers. Louis was slowly trudging up the narrow aisle on the Fifty-Ninth side of the church. Five or six pews before he came to the praying woman, Louis stopped. He looked at her and recognized her. Calling out her name in a single shout, he broke into a struggling stride. Reaching her pew, he leaned in and engulfed the little woman in a huge hug.

"Hi, Mol!" His tremendous smile dribbled over his lips and down his chin.

Startled for just a moment, the woman opened her eyes to see the boy. "Oh, Louis! How good to see you."

"Hi, Mol!" His chubby hand patted her gently on the shoulder. And the old woman, who just a few moments before looked so alone and so pained, was now smiling and laughing. Whatever prayers she was murmuring were answered; whatever pain she was feeling vanished; whatever cross she was carrying was lifted off her fragile shoulders by the special child of God and the special parishioner named Louis.

Some people get angry at God whenever they encounter the spastic and twitching movements of a person like Louis. Why couldn't the all-powerful, the all-good God, who has a reputation for his marvelous handiwork, have made children like Louis "normal like us"? Why couldn't the master universe-builder, who strings the stars in order and brilliance like white pearls in the night sky, dip his hand into all wombs to heal, to bless, and to perfect all his children?

Yet in his own marvelous and mysterious way, God gifts the rest of us with Louis-like children. We need signs! And these "specials of God" are graced with a gift that he has denied the rest of us so-called normal beings: the gift of eternal innocence. To some of us, Louis looks imperfect, but in the Lord's eyes he and his brothers and sisters like him are flawless. They will never offend God as all the rest of us have done. They will never pervert or retard the work of the Father's hands. In a very real sense, children like Louis are necessary to us. They constantly call from us the kindness, the simplicity, the love that keeps us human. They constantly prompt us to prayers of gratitude for our own good health and condition.

And best of all, the Louis-like people of the world have a way of reminding us every day that God is God, that his ways are not ours, and that the smallest fleck of dust in the vastness of his creation never really falls out of his hand.

11

MARGARETTA'S VIEW

**What eye has not seen, and ear has not heard,
and what has not entered the human heart,
what God has prepared for those who love him,
this God has revealed to us through the Spirit
(1 Corinthians 2:9-10).**

It was the last Saturday morning of April and the priest entered
the chrome and glass foyer of the second Bay Ridge Tower. An
awesome wall of nameplates with apartment numbers towered
before him, like the Shea Stadium scoreboard. With his finger he
found the proper plate and pressed the button "24A." The door
burped open and he walked to the elevator where he pushed the
white triangle pointing upward. The plastic triangle immediately
glowed to a dull yellow.

As he waited for the car to arrive, his memory began to flash
images of Margaretta on the screen of his mind. Margaretta's year
had been difficult. First, the doctors had detected cancer, the
inoperable kind, the terrifying kind. Then there were long stints in
New York University Hospital where they ran her through one test

after another, like some appliance on an assembly line. Then came the hated chemotherapy, followed by hair and weight loss.

The elevator door opened like a stage curtain at a Shakespeare tragedy. He entered the empty cab and continued his daydream, not even aware that he had pushed ''24'' on the wall inside the car. It was a lonely, weary, and fearful year for her. She really didn't mind the pain; what bothered her most of all was being dependent, needing help from others. All her life she had been self-reliant, even managed a number of people for a large corporation in the city. Now the roles were switched. This made her uneasy; sometimes it even confused and depressed her.

The elevator rose slowly and the priest leaned against the cold chrome, letting her story play out within him. Whenever any of us receives news of a friend having cancer, he thought, it unsettles us. Gradually it becomes old news and we settle back to the work of our days and weeks. We conveniently hide the ugly, unwelcome news under some rug in our heads. Eventually a final call comes.

''Father John, this is Margaretta. I'm not doing too well. The doctor feels there's some trouble in the liver now. He wants me to check into the hospital again. Could you come down tomorrow so I can go to confession and Communion?''

The elevator stopped at a floor or two on its way to ''24.'' Some people got in but the priest didn't even see them. His memory saw Margaretta stepping up into the pulpit to proclaim the readings at the parish Sunday Masses. And there she was, reverently passing the cup to parishioners with the words ''The Blood of Christ.'' He recalled scenes of her as an officer for the Ladies Auxiliary, sweating through the knots and snags of organizing their annual Communion breakfast. However, the one scene that kept repeating itself was of Margaretta, each weekday morning, kneeling in the fifth or sixth bench for the seven o'clock Mass. She was always well dressed, always healthy looking, always under a fashionable hat.

The priest rode this very same elevator about a year ago when the news first came. That was St. Patrick's Day. The view from her living room and the porch outside was gorgeous. There below them flowed the Narrows spanned by the long bridge, while the sun, like a delicious orange, dangled above the Staten Island horizon.

"God, this must be heaven's view of Brooklyn!" The priest watched the green and red lights punctuating Fourth Avenue all the way to 86th Street. He sounded like a small boy looking down from his first trip on the Wonder Wheel.

"The only bad thing about it, Father, is that I can't see the church. The people across the hall can see the church from their apartment. At night when it's all lit up, it looks like a gem on the hill."

That was just like Margaretta. She loved her church; she loved being in it, she loved being outside and just looking at it.

They celebrated a home Mass together that day. Her hassock became the altar, the end table held the wine, water, and host. He squatted on the footstool while Margaretta, sitting in her lounge chair, proclaimed the readings. She really liked that visit, he thought. All the pain and fear and loneliness were still in her future, but the Eucharist calmed her.

"Whatever happens, Margaretta, don't be afraid. We're with you all the way." He tried to reassure her as he put the cup and cruets into his bag. "What lies before you could very well be the great work of your life. This cancer thing is a tremendous chance for you to do an awful lot of good for so many others. Right now, it's your vocation!"

"I never thought of it that way." She even smiled. "I'll do the best I can, Father."

The elevator daydream switched to a backyard in Long Island. It was a warm summer afternoon and Margaretta was recuperating in her sister's home. Chemotherapy had robbed her of hair, a sour smell of cancer was in the air. Father John had driven a few of her friends out there for a Saturday afternoon visit and lunch together. "How's everyone and everything in the parish?" she asked. "That's the worst thing about this sickness. I miss the church."

The elevator slowed to another stop and a woman, with an embarrassed smile and a small boy, stood there in the hallway. They wanted down, not up, but the child pushed the up button. The priest smiled an OK at them as the chrome curtain slid closed. He continued upward and alone on his journey to "24A." That's when he recalled the spring afternoon visit to Margaretta in the hospital. Once again her room was way up, on the thirty-seventh floor, and once again the view from her window was a tourist's delight: midtown Manhattan stretching silver skyscrapers, the clean blue-black East River muscling its way under the city's bridges.

"Another great view, Margaretta!"

"I know. But it looks uptown. Wish it looked downtown and toward Brooklyn."

"So you could see the church, right?"

"Right!"

The elevator car finally stopped and the numbers over the door were all black except for "24" which glowed. He left the car and made a right to the first door in the hallway — "24A." He pushed the button and waited. For a second he feared he was too late. He rang again. And slowly the door opened and there was Margaretta's smiling silhouette. "I'm so glad you could come, Father."

After a quick hug in the doorway where he could feel her weakness, they sat in the living room again and he let her talk out her heart, her depression. And once again, the Eucharist made her smile. The priest then unleashed a barrage of friendly fire from his arsenal of words that he prayed would destroy her fear, her dejection. As he spoke, he sensed that it was helping. Her eyes looked yellow, her complexion ashen. And past her shoulder, he could see heaven's view of Brooklyn.

The visit ended and it was time to go. As usual she stood in her doorway while he waited for the elevator. "Thank yous" and prayer promises echoed back and forth in the empty corridor. Then came good-bye. The elevator door opened, the priest entered, and he went down.

Two weeks later Margaretta died. And wouldn't you know it, her funeral Mass was in the upper church. During the Mass, he smiled. So much about Margaretta was up. You went up to see her. In a sense, she always called you to come higher. Knowing her was one of life's highs. She always gave you a beautiful view of God and people and parish and life itself. Margaretta was now and forever enjoying heaven's view of Brooklyn — only this time and for all eternity she would see the church.

12

THE DEATHS
OF MIKE HAYDEN

When Jesus arrived [at Bethany], he found that Lazarus had already been in the tomb for four days. Now Bethany was near Jerusalem, only about two miles away. And many of the Jews had come to Martha and Mary to comfort them about their brother. When Martha heard that Jesus was coming, she went to meet him; but Mary sat at home. Martha said to Jesus, "Lord, if you had been here, my brother would not have died. [But] even now I know that whatever you ask of God, God will give you." Jesus said to her, "Your brother will rise." Martha said to him, "I know he will rise, in the resurrection on the last day." Jesus told her, "I am the resurrection and the life; whoever believes in me, even if he dies, will live, and everyone who lives and believes in me will never die" (John 11:17-26).

It was the Sunday after Christmas when Father John heard the news. "Father, did you hear Mike Hayden died?" the Irish brogue repeated it to him while he was greeting the people after Mass.

"Oh, no! Really?" The somber Irish face before him nodded up and down in sad and solemn assent.

"When did it happen?"

"T'other day. Heard it myself from Tommy Raspoli."

"Gee, that's too bad." Father John sighed and said a silent prayer for his good friend, Mike Hayden. Mike came from the same part of the old country as Father's own father. Mike came over here, married Nora, raised a fine family, and settled in the parish. He became an active Holy Name man, an usher, and volunteer for any and every job. His handsome Irish face displayed the warmest smile, his hard hand gave the strongest squeeze, his Irish voice added music to the words he spoke. Just about every day in his life here, he walked up the steep hill of Fifth Avenue to church where he spent most of his time since his Nora died and his married boys moved away. The years took their toll on Mike and, in time, he had trouble seeing. A few years ago he moved in with his son and his family somewhere in Jersey. Father John met him once more after that at a big wake in the parish. He was quite old and feeble and needed his daughter-in-law's arm and eyes to get around.

Father John left the church vestibule and returned to the sacristy where another gray-haired parishioner was waiting for him. "Father, did you hear Mike Hayden died?"

"Yeah, I just heard it from someone in the back vestibule."

"Died in Jersey at his son, Jimmy's. God be good to him."

"Is his funeral going to be here?"

"No, I heard from Martin and Alice Hampton that he was buried already."

"That's too bad. Mike was a great guy. He was a fixture here in the parish for years and years."

Father John took off his vestments and went into the rectory. The elevator door no sooner opened when a priest at the bulletin board greeting him with the now familiar question, ''Did you hear Mike Hayden died?''

''Yeah, I just heard it in church. Did anyone call it in to the office?''

''I don't think so. I heard it in church too. Heard he died in Ohio.''

''Ohio? A lady just told me it was in Jersey.''

''He moved in with Jimmy in Jersey a few years ago but Jimmy moved to Ohio and took Mike with him. He died there.''

''Well, if he died in Ohio,'' Father John surmised, ''I guess there won't be any funeral Mass here.'' The other priest nodded, ''I heard they were going to bury him in Ohio.''

Father John scratched his head. ''I heard he was buried already.'' A tiny doubt surfaced in his mind about the news of Mike's death. Too many different and varied facts were coming in. However, all day long, wherever he went, all he heard was the greeting that was taking the place of ''Merry Christmas'' or ''Happy New Year.'' People looked at him and immediately announced, ''Father, did you hear Mike Hayden died?'' It just had to be true. Too many people knew about it. The IT&T (the Irish Telephone and Telegraph) system of communication has never been known to be anything but reliable, accurate, and, in fact, infallible. Even though the details of Mike's death were varied — some said he died in Ohio, others said New Jersey; some said he was already buried, others said in a few days; some said he died at his son's home, others said in a rest home — Father John accepted the fact that his friend since he was a boy was now with the angels. God be good to him.

On New Year's Eve, Father John wrote Mike's name on the list of deceased people to be prayed for at all the holy day Masses. Mike should be prayed for by the parishioners, he thought. After all, Mike was a pillar of this parish for decades.

So at all the Masses on the first day of the year, Mike Hayden's name was called out by each lector as one of our recently deceased. And the people paused in silence to present his name, other names, and all their intentions to the Lord. Parishioner after parishioner came to the rectory office to have Masses offered for Mike. Mass cards were written. Different societies and old-time friends came to the rectory window and said to Brother Tom, "It's a shame about Mike Hayden. May I have a Mass card please?" And Brother scribbled his name in the big book and on the small cards while the prayers of white-headed companions rose before the shrine and the tabernacle, pleading God to be good to their old friend, Mike Hayden.

And God was so good to Mike that on the fourth day of the new year, Father John received a unique phone message from Akron, Ohio. The message simply read: "Jimmy Hayden called. His father is *not* dead." Just as Father John suspected in the first place. A wild rumor, with no confirmation, about someone's death turned out to be just a rumor after all.

A mixed assortment of feeling swept over Father John. Of course he was happy that Mike Hayden was alive again. The phone message had the joy of a birth announcement. He also laughed out loud as he imagined poor Jimmy Hayden and his wife receiving Mass card after Mass card and scores of sympathy cards over the recent death of his father, who was sitting before them all at the supper table enjoying his potatoes. Mike Hayden would now be able to use the words of Mark Twain: "The recent reports of my death have been grossly exaggerated."

Although Father John felt happy and giddy, he sensed a shadow of sadness because Mike would have to die again — only next time it would be for real. Mike became a latter-day Lazarus. Poor Mike. Will the people believe it when he really dies? Will they pray as hard for him? What is God going to do with all those Masses offered for the repose of the soul of a man who isn't reposing at all, but alive and well in Akron, Ohio?

Then panic set in. How in the world was Father John going to notify all the parishioners that Mike Hayden was alive? He would set out on his travels around the parish and tell as many parishioners as he could "Mike Hayden isn't dead!" Invariably he would get as a response, "Sure he is, Father. His name was announced from the pulpit on New Year's day." Convincing the people that Mike Hayden was alive would be harder than raising the dead back to life.

So on Sunday morning, Father John announced the strange but good news to the women at the monthly Communion breakfast of the Ladies Auxiliary. "On Wednesday, Mike Hayden was prayed for at all the Masses as being deceased. Well, I found out yesterday that this was untrue. Mike is not dead. He was just sick." The ladies at first laughed and then applauded. One woman yelled out "Sure, it's the power of prayer." Another remarked, "Why that's the first time a man went from the deceased list to the sick list." The ladies received the news with joy and promised that they would spread the good news around. "Sure, we certainly know how to pray a man back to life in this parish, don't we?"

When all was said and done there was no harm done at all. Mike Hayden got himself talked about and remembered and prayed for. Even though the word was out that he died, Mike certainly didn't feel any pain. And it was interesting for a change to hear the news going around the parish that someone was alive. So often Father John hears only about so-and-so who died. However, in the future, whenever he gets told about a friend or parishioner dying, he'll think twice and pray twice and remember the day that Mike Hayden died — and came to life again. Because that's really what is going to happen to all of us, isn't it?

13

THE MAN WITH GOD'S EAR

Whoever does not carry his own cross and come after me cannot be my disciple (Luke 14:27).

The pink phone message simply read "Woman would like confession and Communion for her husband who is sick." There was also a name, an address, and a phone number scribbled on the top of the note so Father John went right to his phone and dialed the number.

"Hello, this is Father John. You called about confession and Communion for your husband?"

"Yes, Father. But there's no emergency. My husband has been sick for some time and we thought it would be good if he had confession and Communion."

"OK, I'll be there in twenty minutes. Are you on the first floor or upstairs?"

"First floor, Father. But there's no real hurry."

"OK, see you in a half hour."

And that was how Father John met Mr. Jim Tobin. It started with a simple September sick call. Mr. Tobin lay stretched on top of the well-made bed in the back bedroom. He wore his flannel pajamas covered by a warm, cozy-looking bathrobe. Friendly features — a pointed chin and nose highlighted by bright, lively eyes — marked a fine face topped by neatly parted angel-white hair. Here was a man in his late seventies, a man who had lived, worked, and raised a family from this very house, a man who wanted the holy sacraments, a man who was dying of cancer. Here was a man with God's ear.

Father John sat at the bottom of the bed and the two of them chatted and smiled. Mr. Tobin was in the prime of his life when Father John was a kid running these streets. The two different histories came together on that cloudy September morn. The altar boy and the lunch-pail laborer of forty years ago met as the sick septuagenarian and as the holy oil and Eucharist-carrying parish priest. First came confession, "Through the ministry of the Church may God give you pardon and peace," then came the anointing, "Through this holy anointing may the Lord in his love and mercy help you with the grace of the Holy Spirit," and then came the Eucharist, "The Body of Christ." To which the old man amened! Then Mrs. Tobin came into the room and joined them in their conversation of parish and family and the old days.

"You know, Father, all we wanted was confession and Communion anytime today. But you didn't have to come. Anyone could have come over," Mrs. Tobin remarked. "You must be terribly busy."

Father John always smiled when people said things like that. As if he was the only one who was busy and the other priests weren't. As if the Jesus in the Eucharist that he brought was a better Jesus than the Eucharist the other priests brought on their sick calls.

"Oh, no trouble at all," Father John responded. "I enjoy coming out of the rectory and getting away from bills and phone calls and salesmen. This is the best part of being a parish priest."

They chatted some more and, as he was leaving, Father John said he would look in again and keep an eye on his new friend, Mr. Tobin.

The months passed and it became evident that Mr. Tobin was running out of days. But one of his nicest days was Christmas day. On that morning Father John walked between snow flurries to his old friend's house to bring him Jesus for Christmas. Mr. Tobin sat in the front room that morning, right next to his Christmas tree. The house was warm and smelled of turkey and turnips, and Mrs. Tobin beamed in her holiday apron. The old man looked happy, but it was obvious to Father John that he had failed and had lost a few pounds.

A son was already at the house, and a daughter, with her family, would be arriving later. The family members joined in with the prayers and a solemn silence came over the happy room when Mr. Tobin received his Christmas Communion. It was the beginning of a good day and a happy Christmas, even though it was to be his last December 25th alive.

The dark days of winter dragged along like an Eskimo lost in a blizzard. Occasionally Father John would meet Mr. Tobin's wife who recounted how he was in and out of the hospital. A winter thaw arrived in mid-February with a blast of blazing sunshine. That was when Father John received another pink phone message.

"Hello, this is Father John. How's he doing?"

"He's in Victory Memorial. He's having trouble breathing but he's asking for you. Wants to go to confession."

"I'll be there this afternoon."

A few hours later Father John found the hospital room and there was his friend, lying on the bed in his warm, cozy robe. An oxygen mask covered his mouth and nose. He looked so fragile, so thin, but when he saw Father John a huge smile creased his face beneath the plastic mask. His wife stood next to the bed holding on to his bony hand.

Father John repeated the final sacraments: the forgiving blessing, the healing anointing, the precious Bread. And the three of them enjoyed their final chat.

"He wouldn't give me any peace till you came, Father. I told him that since yesterday was Ash Wednesday and the beginning of Lent you were very busy. But he kept pestering me to call you."

A big smile danced on Mr. Tobin's face. He was even beginning to look better, as if the sacraments were the medicine he needed.

"Are you in any pain, Jim?" Father John asked.

"No, I feel fine. Really."

"Well, I'll be away for a week. As soon as I come back, I'll stop in to see you but not in the hospital. I want to visit you at home, not here."

"I'd love to be out of here myself," Mr. Tobin sighed.

"I'll be praying for you, but I want you to pray for me." Father John was asking his friend for a favor.

"You want me to pray for you?" Mr. Tobin's eyes widened. "Ha! You don't need my prayers. I need yours."

Father John marveled at how good were people like the husband and wife before him and how little they realized it. Oh, if they only could get a glimpse of how special they are and how much God loves them, he thought.

"Listen, Jim. Anyone suffering with a serious disease, anyone sick in the hospital is carrying a very choice cross, but he also has the ear of God." Father John was serious. "So say a prayer for me. You have God's ear."

The couple both laughed and Mrs. Tobin came back with . . . "If Jim has God's ear, Father, then you must have the rest of God's body." That remark even struck Father John as funny. There was no way that he could convince these wonderful people how good and precious they were to God.

"Well, promise you'll say a prayer for me, Jim." The priest held the fragile fingers of his friend in a final handshake.

"See you when I get back."

That was the last time the old gentleman and his friend, the priest, ever saw each other again. Since he was having trouble eating the hospital food, his wife went home that night to make him some soup.

"Don't bother," the husband told the wife, "I might not be here when you come back." And he wasn't. The next morning the man who had the ear of God was enjoying God's company, face-to-face.

A week passed and Father John came home to find out that his friend had died the day after he visited and sacramented him on that hospital afternoon. The news of his death hurt, but that he missed his wake and funeral Mass pained him the most. He reached for the phone and called his old friend's wife.

"I'm so sorry. I just heard the news."

"Oh, Father. He went very fast. Once he got those final sacraments, it was like he knew he was ready to go, so off he went. He was only waiting for you to come with the absolution, the holy oil, and the Communion. Then he was ready, so he left quietly and quickly." There was a smile in the sound of her voice.

They chatted on the phone together and Father John heard all the details of the wake, the Mass, and the burial.

"I'll really miss him," he told her. "I used to enjoy our visits. However, I can still talk to him whenever I want because he really has God's ear now."

She laughed, thanked him for everything, and hung up. A week or two later a small box for Father John arrived at the rectory. Inside was a pyx for carrying the Blessed Sacrament on sick calls. On the back was engraved "IN MEMORY OF JAMES J. TOBIN." Father John smiled and squeezed the circular gold case in his hand. The man with God's ear would travel with him on future sacramental trips to all the other wonderful people who also have God's ear.

More from Liguori Publications

THE PARABLES OF JESUS
20 Stories With a Message
by Daniel L. Lowery, C.SS.R.

This book helps readers get in touch with the important message behind the principal parables found in Luke's Gospel. Includes questions for reflection to help readers consider the meaning of the parables in the context of contemporary life. **$1.95**

THROUGH A FATHER'S EYES
Stories of Life and Love
by Tom Sheridan

This collection of stories contains the memories, the experiences, the life and love of a father. Here you will touch the essence of fatherhood, the specialness of what it means to be a male parent. **$1.95**

THE ROAD HOME
Five True Stories of Catholics Who Returned to the Church
by Mark Neilsen

Here are five Catholics who struggled with faith, God, and religion and left the Church. The stories of why they returned tell us so much about the workings of the human heart and about the grace of God. **$2.95**

DOWN GOSPEL BYWAYS
18 Stories of People Who Met Jesus
by Mary Terese Donze, A.S.C.

In this book you will share the loves, learn of the hopes and fears, and touch the One who touched the lives of people who knew Jesus. More than just a collection of interesting short stories, this book offers "creative aids to those who base their prayer life on the Gospels." **$2.95**

Order from your local bookstore or write to:
Liguori Publications, Box 060, Liguori, Missouri 63057
*(Please add 75¢ for postage and handling for first
item ordered and 25¢ for each additional item.)*